we have everything we need to start again

we have everything we need to start again

koleka putuma

illustrated by **Adriana Bellet**

HOT KEY BOOKS

First published in Great Britain in 2024 by
HOT KEY BOOKS
4th Floor, Victoria House, Bloomsbury Square
London WC1B 4DA
Owned by Bonnier Books
Sveavägen 56, Stockholm, Sweden
bonnierbooks.co.uk/HotKeyBooks

Text copyright © Koleka Putuma, 2024
Illustrations copyright © Adriana Bellet, 2024

All rights reserved.
No part of this publication may be reproduced, stored or transmitted in any form or by any means, electronic, mechanical, photocopying or otherwise, without the prior written permission of the publisher.

The right of Koleka Putuma and Adriana Bellet to be identified as author and illustrator of this work has been asserted by them in accordance with the Copyright, Designs and Patents Act 1988.

This is a work of fiction. Names, places, events and incidents are either the products of the author's imagination or used fictitiously. Any resemblance to actual persons, living or dead, is purely coincidental.

A CIP catalogue record for this book is available from the British Library.

ISBN: 978-1-4714-1332-2

Also available as an ebook and in audio

1

Typeset by Michelle Brackenborough

Printed and bound in Great Britain by Clays Ltd, Elcograf S.p.A.

MIX
Paper | Supporting responsible forestry
FSC® C018072

Hot Key Books is an imprint of Bonnier Books UK
bonnierbooks.co.uk

*For you, I hope what you are looking for
has already found you.*

Contents

Prologue   1

Part 1 *We are learning new names.*
(Don't) Mind the Language	5
Direct Message	9
Pro Noun	15
Braveheart	21
Coming Out	25
YOLO	26
Intersection	28
Inhalant	31
Chalk Outline	35
Lifeline	36
Balance Beam	38
Home	43
Braeburn	44
Stories	47
Roots	48
Google	51

Part 2 *If not today...*
To Earth, with Love.	57
Chatbot	58
Release	60
Father Where?	64
Sea Legs	66
Weighing-In	68
Elastic	70
Two Left Feet	73

Present	74
I Thought	77
Uprising	78
Teachings	80
Today Peaceful, Tomorrow Warlike, The Next Day Warlike Again.	82
Refuge	87
Banned/Burned	88
Boundaries	91
Passage	92

Part 3 ... *then tomorrow.*

History	99
Homecoming	100
Protégé or Prototype	103
Kid Gloves	106
Pinky Promise	109
Unlearning	110
Speak	112
Pause	114
F is for Forgiveness	117
SoundCloud	118
Odyssey	120
Meteor (or Masculinity)	122
Choice Assorted	124
Roll Call	127
Twenty-One Ways to Check Your Pulse	129
Praise Poem	139

Epilogue   141

Prologue

You are the light at the end of the tunnel.

Part 1

We are learning new names.

(Don't) Mind the Language

TikTok,
the advanced Google,

tallies the minutes we spend minding
each other's business

Thesauruses
captured in captions

communicate what and
how it is read

Captcha tells
us apart from our computers

There is no limit to the number of characters
that share our story

Screenshot
has made free speech costly

Cultures want to cancel
what they have cultivated

We have created currencies
that cannot be converted to life (or living)

In our world

Voice notes are how we read each other
and tone is more than a colour

Not all meaning can be found in what is said
What is said sometimes means the opposite of what is sent

The internet does not forget
Signals are not lost in translation

Ellipses have us on the edge of our fingertips

always waiting for *typing* . . .
to become something.

Direct Message

single
unpunctuated
phrases
are how we keep it
caszh

as in
you don't want to come across as too eager

as in
i'm as chilled as a sentence without punctuation

as in
full sentences are recipes for anxiety

as in
don't leave too many silences between texting

as in
don't message too often or too long or never at all

as in
overthinking will always live rent-free

as in
fr.

as in
for real

as in
the lies we tell ourselves
are as tricky as the truths we do not face

as in
your *L*s do not determine your *W*s

as in
PERIODTTTTTT

as in
!

as in
end of discussion

as in
my mother uses my full name when she is angry

as in
iykyk

as in
you do not want this smoke

as in
fire shows us where it's lit

as in
LIT

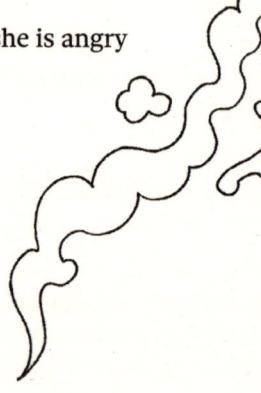

as in
iconic

as in
major

as in
slay

as in
🏃‍♀️

as in
giving me life

as in
i'm living

as in
i'm here for it

as in
spill the tea

as in
pull out the receipts

as in
facts

as in
BIG FACTS
no printer

as in
we are digital and alive

as in
online

as in
IRL

as in
algospeak is the language of our algorithms

as in
we spell phonetically to avoid censorship

as in
we cannot be silenced

as in
we take up space

as in
being EXTRA!

as in
TYPING IN ALL CAPS is how we show enthusiasm

as in
highkey we are passionate about being passionate

as in
lowkey we are always in our feelings

as in
🥺

as in
we keep in touch to stay in touch

as in
HMU

as in
language doesn't mind how it slides,
it just loves to dance.

Pro Noun

Westerford High School in Cape Town brings the country's education system into the present. Students have the choice to wear a badge showcasing their own pronouns on it.

i.

Teacher uses my pronoun
while mispronouncing my name.

What remains after a change
is what refuses to stay the same.

Pro-this.
Pro-that.

Progressing.
Progressive.

Lola is transitioning.
Sam is on antidepressants.

Code of conduct states
[x]phobia is prohibited.

But uniforms are limited
to dresses and trousers.

We look for mirrors in books,
search for selves in browsers.

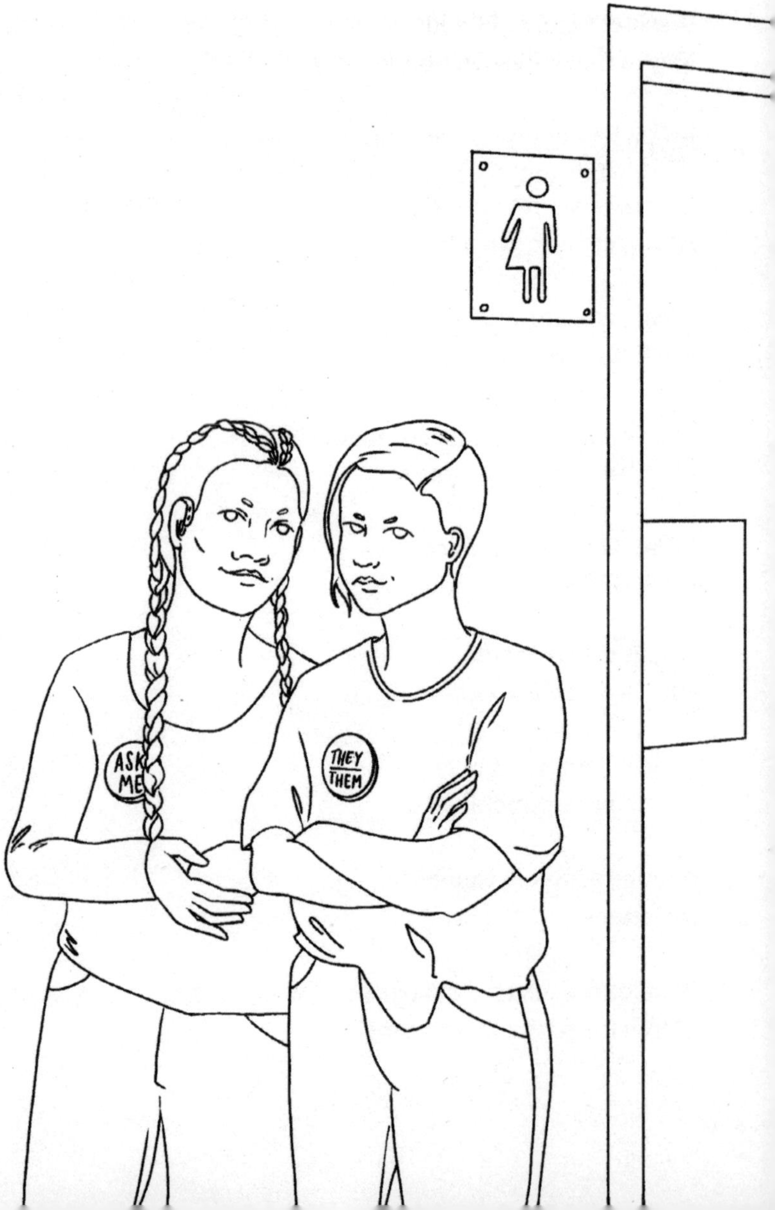
ASK ME
THEY THEM

Must keep tabs on pop culture
while fashioning subculture.

Webster dictionary adds
they to the definition of non-binary.

From delinquents to law-abiding citizens,
those who embrace love will be counted as witnesses.

One day,

restroom lines won't care where I stand
as long as I piss and wash my hands,

I'll say I'm neither this nor that.
Grandma will understand.

Won't be afraid to voice
I'm [beep] and I'm proud

To be anything and everything,

> *I'm allowed, I'm allowed.*

ii.

Hoodie, sneakers, Lil Nas through the speakers.
They won't have to wear layers to cover the procedure,

won't have to wear a sign
to be legible for the reader,

won't be afraid to be
outside of the line,

won't be out of line by being
off-centre,

won't be a spectacle
by bending gender,

won't need permission
to be

won't need permission.

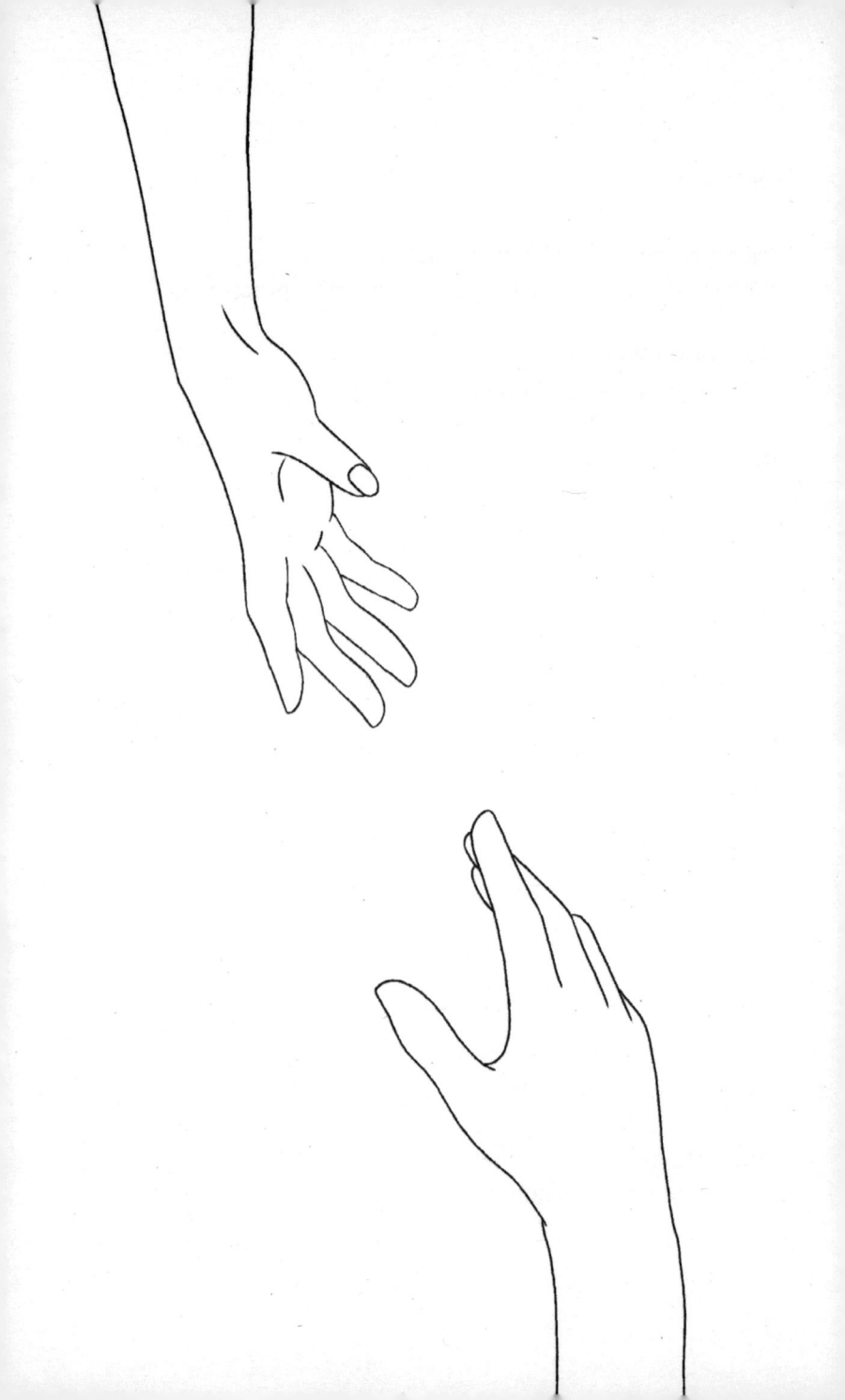

Braveheart

Before puberty claimed my body
I kissed Fran,

slow and clumsy,
it was weird, and fascinating enough

to try again.

She was a desire that taught me
that you don't need to lower your eyes when you say the words

bipolar

or

gay.

You can lift your throat and your spine
to bring yourself into a room.

For us, consent meant being sure.
I know now,

we all deserve the kind of want
that insists on being sure.

The first time I kissed Lihle
he asked if I had a condom.

He was the first experiment to teach me
that some boys assume silence means yes.

My first heartbreak left on a bus,

left me with a voicemail and
feelings of distrust.

I thought the tornado would never stop spinning.

A character in the last movie I watched said
'taking a break' is breaking up for cowards.

I wonder if being a coward
is the opposite of *not being sure*.

Fran would say,

*Sometimes we are brave,
sometimes we are afraid.*

What I know of bravery is that
I still choose to be here,

I still choose to wish for infinite love,

for a love that doodles in maths exams,
passes notes in a muted library.

A love that feels like a freebie in a goodie bag,
an unexpected gift in a lucky packet.

Feels like my favourite playlist
on a bad day.

That has the courage to call a break
by what it needs.

I want a love

that will remind me of
how vast time can be,

how long a breath can stretch.

A love that says
brave and *afraid* can sometimes feel the same.

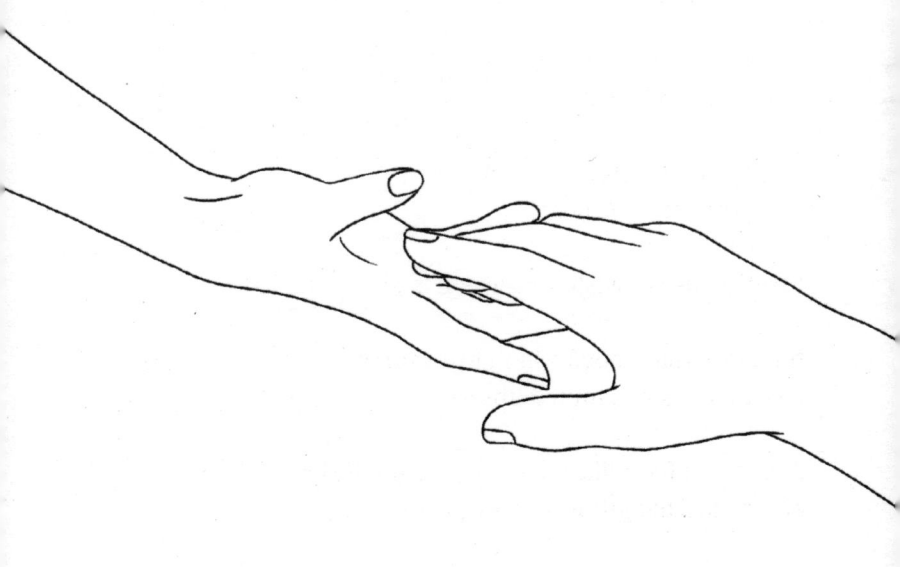

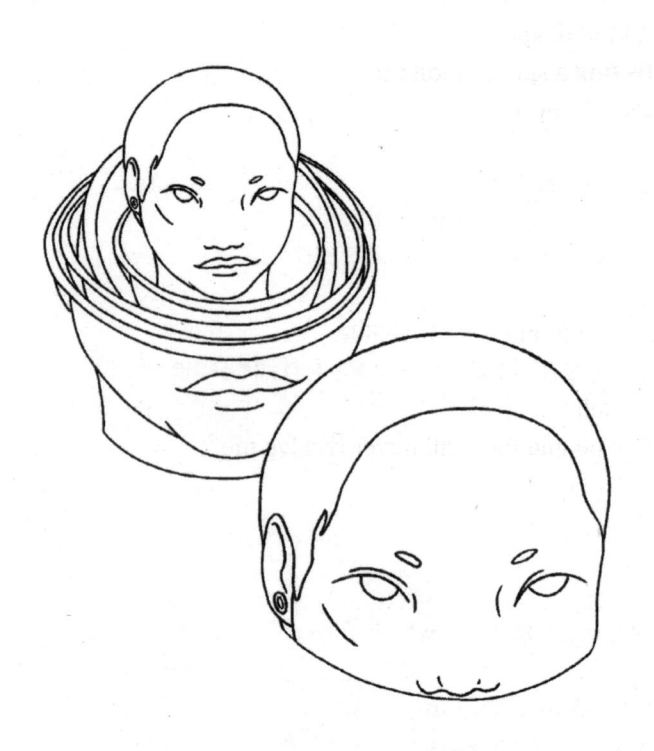

Coming Out

It's a kind of skill:
hoarding multiple lives in one body.

It's a kind of sport:
perfecting a split persona to
protect the peace.

I have learned how
to speak in a voice that muffles.

I move with/in
facades that make me invisible.

I trace self
back to people that will never receive me

as I am.

I am learning home is where freedom is.
I am learning home is where love is.

Some of us lose our kin
when we call ourselves
by our names.

YOLO

We huddle,
spirits and ouid in one hand,
iPhone of the Year in the other,

serotonin injecting our self-worth.

We live in reels of lives
always *Live*, and seldom
living,

Euphoria-inspired fits purchased off Shein
with money for buses and books.

Sephora skincare and hand-poked tattoos
hidden under overpriced hoodies

we are profiled in.

We dance awkwardly,
glancing over our shoulders,

scouting for something better,
not far from where we are having a good time.

Insta-famous is a currency.
Blue tick is *it*.

We sell ourselves as
carefully constructed online figures,

fabricate realities for the gram.

We are liked for what we don't show.
We must be followed to be seen.

Intersection

At the intersection
we are the opposite of the same.

At the intersection
our afflictions meet,

sometimes our eyes do not.

At the intersection
we choose what to see,

who to greet,

who is deserving of our grace,
our time.

At the intersection
we bring our theories

but sometimes forget to bring our hearts –
we get close from a distance.

At the intersection
we intellectualise the things that brought us here;

all the things we are,
all the things we are not allowed to be.

At the intersection
we learn to make allies of our enemies.

At the intersection
there is always room for misunderstanding.

At the intersection
we observe before we cross

each other,
or cross-examine each other.

At the intersection
some of us are profiled
while others are seen for who they are.

At the intersection
grey areas are reserved for pause.

At the intersection
freedom and oppression cannot co-exist.

At the intersection
all suffering is connected.

At the intersection
we are black and white and mixed and queer and ill and well
and thriving and poor and lists and numbers and people and
spirit and body and present and passing and religious and
agnostic and inside and out and—

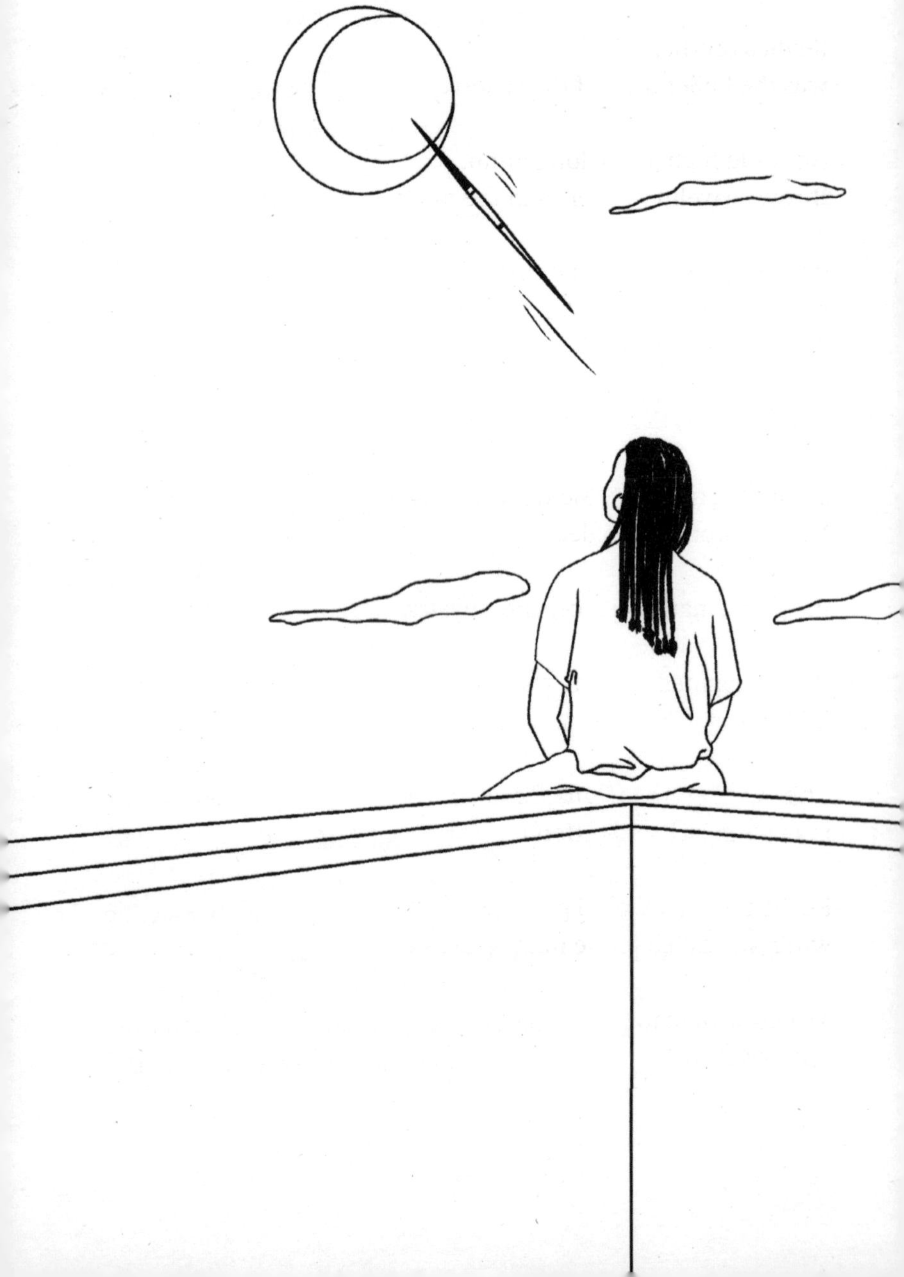

Inhalant

Kevin's brother
was the bullet train of the school.

He could high jump, long jump,
throw a javelin further than the moon.

Before he dropped out of ninth grade
he would get straight A's.

Everything changed
when Kevin's brother got expelled,

before the unspeakable word
Kevin's brother excelled

in sports, math, science, and physics.

They imagined one day watching him
in the Olympics.

This was before the unspeakable word
made him sick and different.

Kevin's mother would grab the air
when she called to the man in the sky.

Armed with fear
and scripture,

this ritual became a lullaby.

Kevin's mother arrived at the foot of the cross,
with knees worn from bending,

her tongue curled around the mecca of chaos,
bargaining with any god who was good at

performing miracles,

she was too busy praying to notice.
Heaven was experiencing technical difficulties.

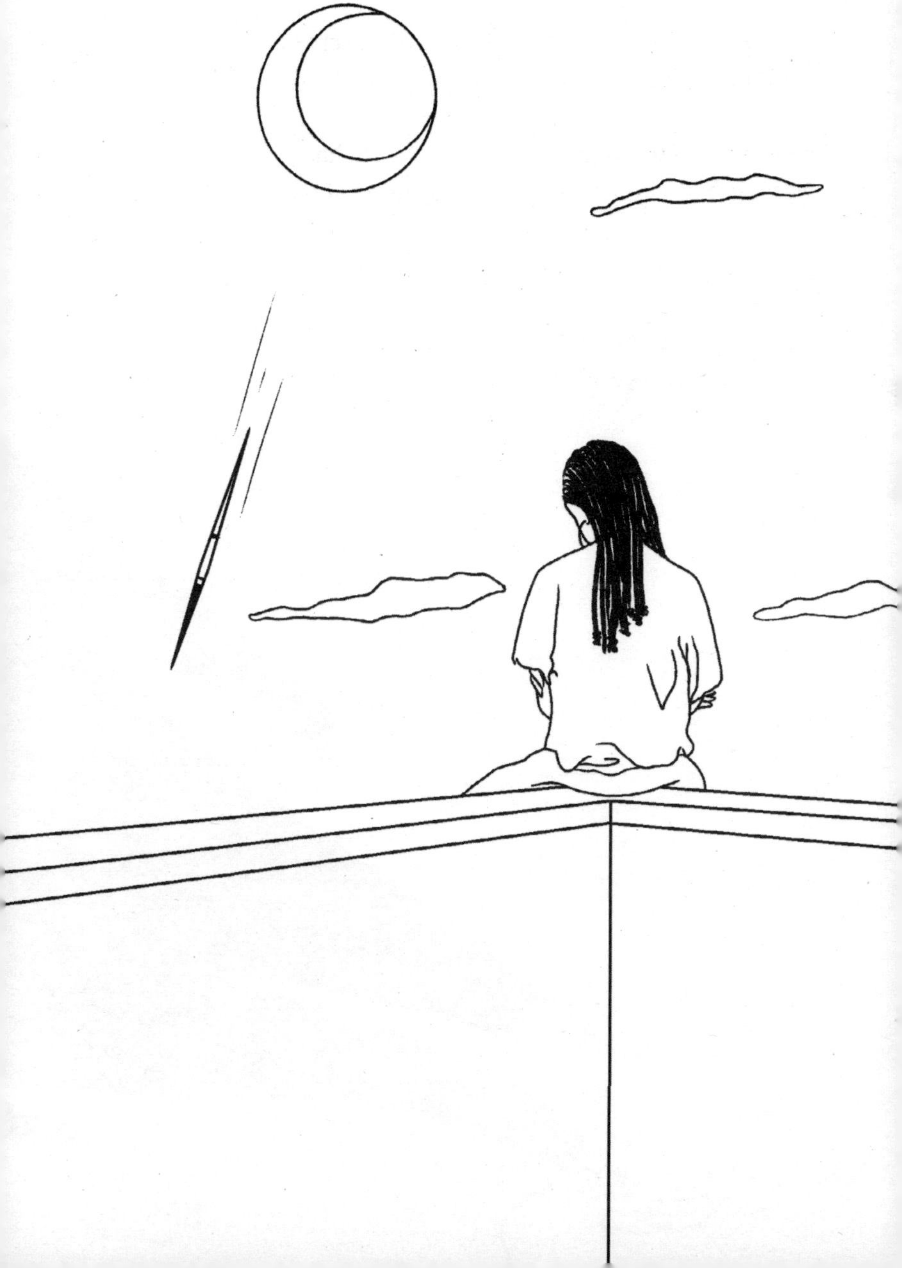

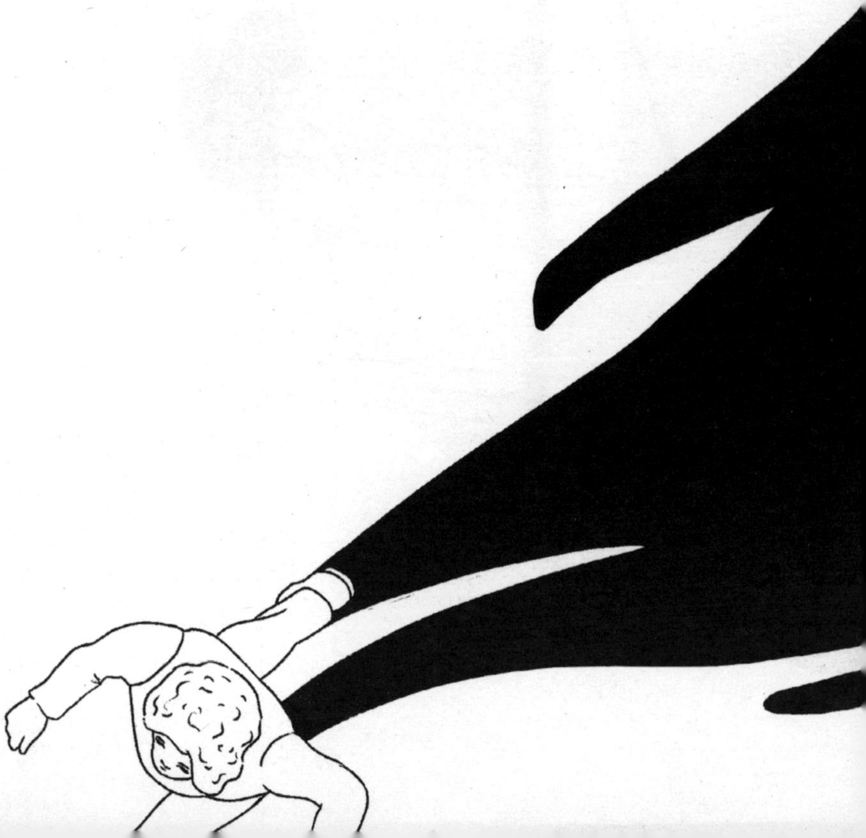

Chalk Outline

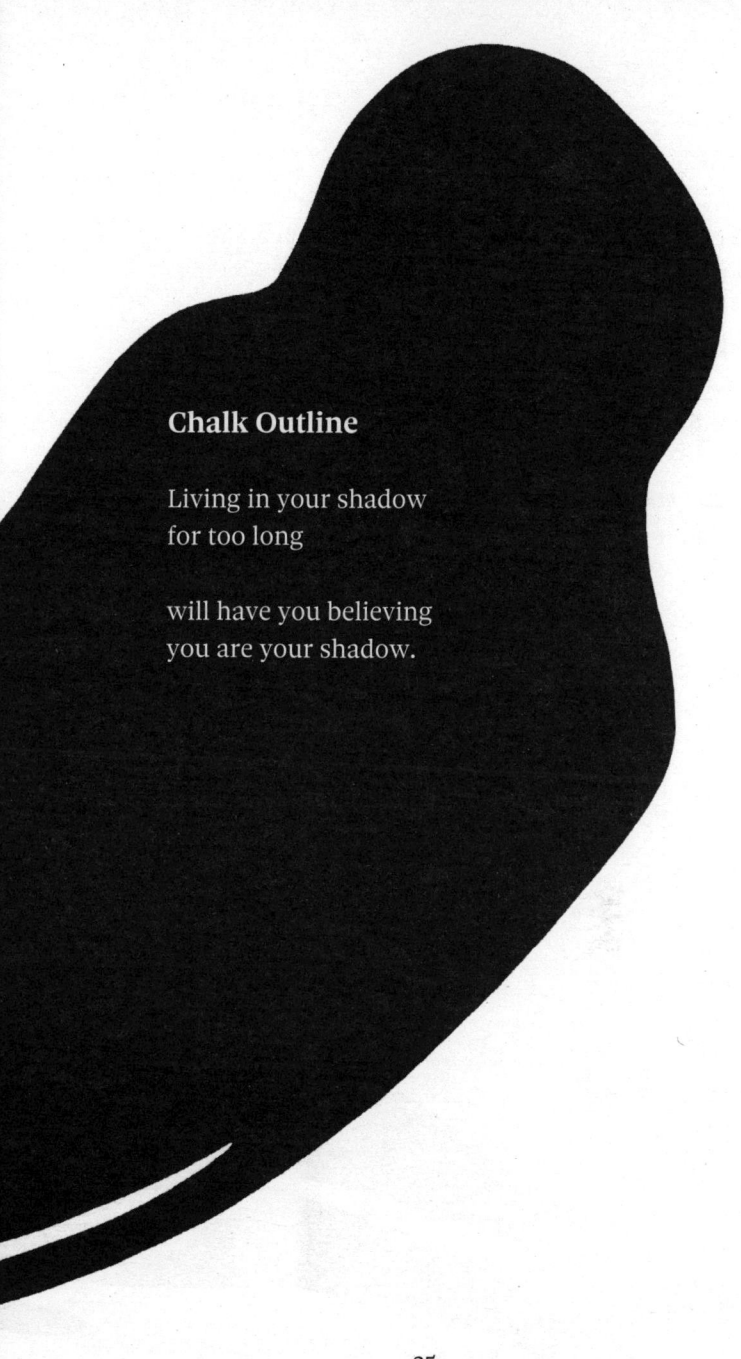

Living in your shadow
for too long

will have you believing
you are your shadow.

Lifeline

Blood can make you realise how thick water can be.
Make family or *familiar* where you can;

kin is kin.

There will always be somewhere to return to.

Wherever you find the water,
know that it is strong enough to carry you.

Balance Beam

When we were little,
we put the gymnasts on TV to shame.

Backbend, bridge, handstand, backward roll – onlookers
choreographing our bodies into a spectacle.

Observers,
calculating our steps, applauding our flexibility.

Our bones were loose and reckless
before the unforeseen danger,

before we were taught to have eyes
at the back of our paranoia,

to be skeptical of strangers who are too nice.

Now we are accustomed to running

                                          in our sleep.

We are accustomed to saying sorry,
pardoning ourselves even when we do not need to be excused.

When our bodies grew around,
in between places,

we started learning all the names
we didn't want to be called when we moved.

Protruding bellies were cautionary tales – horrors
of what happens to flesh that straddles,

                                    s p l i t s,

and arches for pleasure.

As if only for or in pleasure
are we wayward.

As if pleasure is a dirty word.
Our grandmothers parted grounds in search of a home
without traitors.

We are tethered to our mother
and her mother's shame.

We inhabit the memory until it feels like home,
our bed is already pressed for us to lie in.

We are torsos that can be snapped and shredded until the
ground swallows us
out there and in here.

We have seen limbs like ours
tossed in the air for sport,

for pleasure

                not ours.

As if that kind and this kind of dancing are reason enough
to pardon being watched,

followed until you transmit fear into every movement.

You deserve to be believed
when you say it happened to you.

Bare-flesh dancing is too sacred
to be looked upon with shame.

      We learn new ways of moving
      to learn new names.

           We are learning new names.

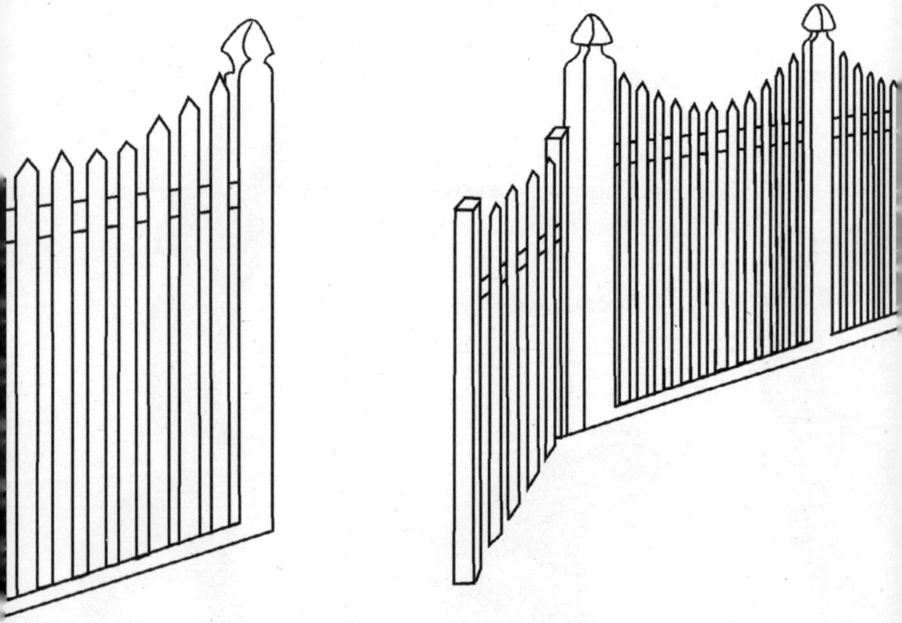

Home

I search for myself in all the places
I have ever loved.

This is evidence that I belonged somewhere,
however brief.

I've run out of anecdotes
to describe home,

I've run out of antidotes
that make being home bearable.

I survive being gay
in all the places they said it was not allowed,

I survive the looming threat of disappearing
while no one is looking.

Braeburn

I am an apple that has fallen
from a tree uprooted by the wind,

its stems carrying promises of birthdays,
and holidays.

A polaroid always developing,
never quite the picture.

For as long as I have known you,
you have never wanted to be known.

You come and go as you please.

Things in the wind are fragile,
unpredictable.

You and your dead colours—
what hue were you before?

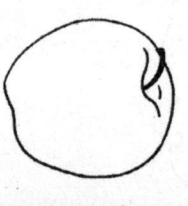

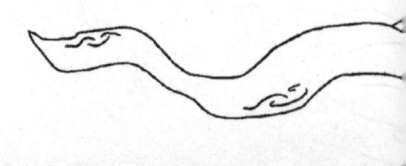

Your father, my grandfather,
was uprooted by many wars;

you, from us,
by drinking too much poison and wandering.

What names did you answer to
before you were called breadwinner or provider?

Which seasons brought you here?
Why do some seasons make you absent?

Stories

I carry hauntings
that belong to other people.

Greedy and demanding,
there is always a story that is unsatisfied.

How many stories find their way home,
find their time?

Some stories announce themselves, wild and boastful:

It's my time! It's my time! It's my time!

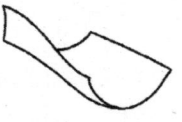

Others will always be waiting for their time to come.

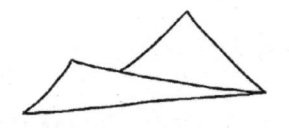

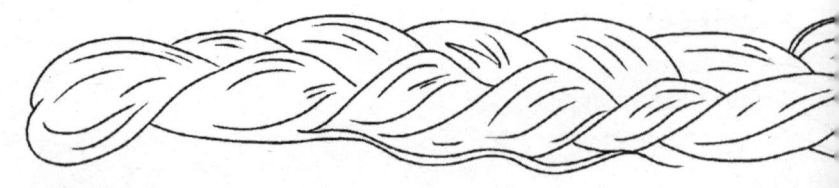

Roots

Like cornrows named after cornfields,
Like canerows in the Caribbean,
Like cascading wave inches,
Like sculptural mohawks defying gravity,

Like head wraps adorned with beads: an act of rebellion against oppression,

Like shells paying homage to Fulani coiffures in West Africa,
Like Ghanaian dukus and doeks in South Africa,
Like Bantu knots stretched into sections,
Like hip-length box braids call out to eembuvi braids of the Mbalantu women in Namibia,

Like nappy coils curled in kinks and twists,
Like twisted locs locked in,
Like microlocs and nappylocs and sisterlocks interlocked at the root, rooting for you
Like sisterlockticians,

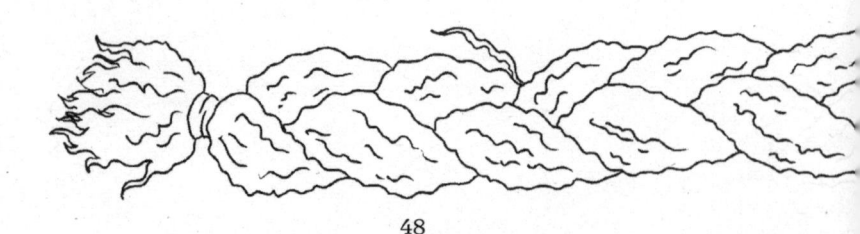

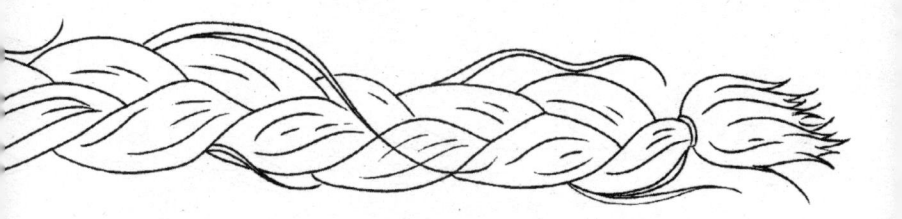

Like grassroots natural hair movements,
Like Senegalese twists twisted around afros,

Like retro, disco-funk, and soulful,
Like nostalgia, nostalgic
Like Bo Derek braids and Willow whipping her hair back and forth,

Like puffs and pixie cut,
Like a fade, faded like dead-ends on washdays,

Like "distracting", "unpresentable", "untidy", "unprofessional", "inappropriate",
Like at work, in schools, in the streets,

Like *Don't Touch My Hair,*
Like every strand is an anchor to history.

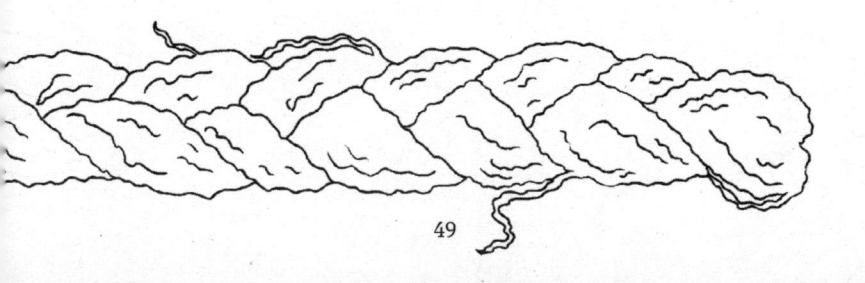

Google

> *How to transition?*

Beginnings and endings bring us here.

> *How to feminism?*

It must and must always honour all freedoms.

> *How to dismantle patriarchy?*

Its teachings begin where things are first taught.

> *How to stand up?*

What are the hills you are prepared to die on,
do they crucify others?

> *How to stand out?*

Our wildest hopes are wrapped up in our fears.

> *How to be?*

Sometimes fitting in hinders us from standing out.

> *How to feel comfortable in your own skin?*

Love is where we meet ourselves.

> *How to love?* 🔍

Not knowing is a beautiful place to be.

> *How to ground yourself?* 🔍

When you are not present on your own journey, you miss out on so much.

> *How to let reality suck?* 🔍

Do not attempt to put anything in its place.

> *How to release?* 🔍

Use every limb in the limbos between,
forward and forward,

letting go of what you need to let go.

> *How to let go?* 🔍

You have survived everything you have feared, so what are you afraid of?

> *How to become?* 🔍

Nothing is linear.

> *How to dream?*

Befriend your impostor monsters.

> *How to make friends?*

Make this an ongoing exploration with self.

> *How to make your parents proud?*

It counts that you are proud of yourself, too.

> *How to predict the future?*

Everything is in its season.

> *How to change the world?*

You owe your dreams your courage.

Part 2

If not today . . .

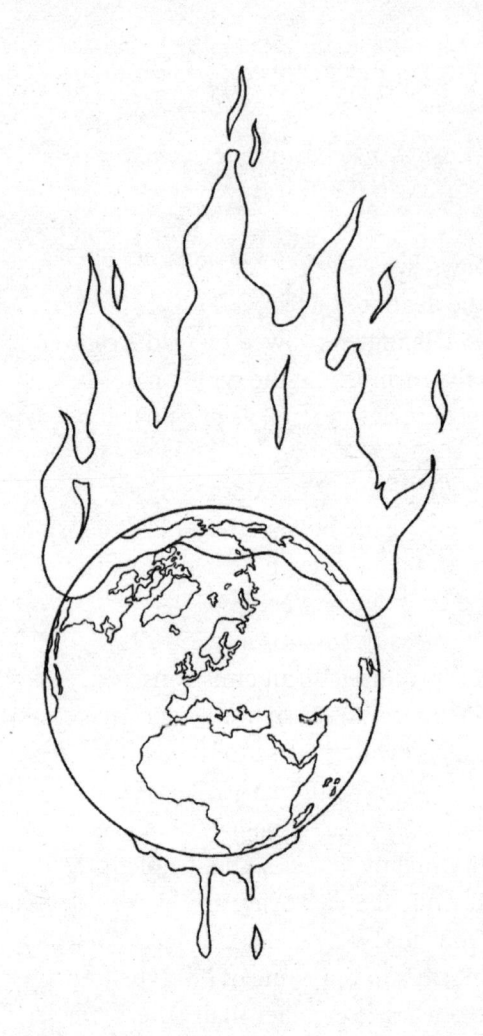

* From a report compiled by the World Meteorological Organization

To Earth, with Love.

Climate-related disasters have increased fivefold over the past five decades.*

read the news, we
measure the death toll, we
watch the TV being swallowed by wildfires, we
hold onto the furniture in the typhoon, we
migrate to countries that tell us to go back to where it burns, we
sink with sand, we
witness how gravel caves underwater, we
send kind regards to Pakistan, Nigeria, and Kwa-Zulu Natal, we
separate from the world, we
undertake a tech detox, we
call on rich polluting countries, we
believe their promises to cut emissions, we
demand the minimum from our leaders, we
vote for leaders who promise to lead, we
pray for those without homes while we
eat gnocchi under solar-panelled roofs, we
vow to quit praising virtue-signaling pledges, we
fall behind while they innovate ahead, we
dry up all the taps, we
thaw the glaciers in the name of the expedition, we
regard some wars as deadlier than others, we
keep up with the kardashians, we
starve while eating the rich, we

explode before the eyes of god, we—

Chatbot

Sleep-deprived bones,
nervous systems on edge,

the future is always calling us
into the present.

We are missed calls and notifications
on high alert.

We trend
in the past tense, arrive

already tired.

We are made under pressure in
pressure cookers.

We cannot BeReal with a filter,
we filter intimacy through memes and GIFs,

slide into conversations
wearing our emojis on our sleeves.

Ghosting is how we communicate our presence.

Our devices keep us dis/connected,
bombarded by something new always going viral.

We are viral, spread thin

by demands to be everything
everywhere, all at once.

We are applications running in the background,
depleted by always being on, and on

Tik
Tok
       Tik
       Tok,

anxiety at the dinner table.

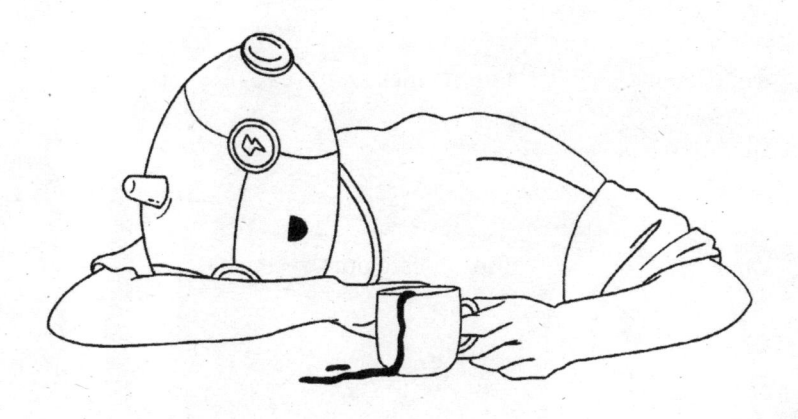

Release

worn.

wearing. weary.

wry. wrought. wrong.

robbed. raw.

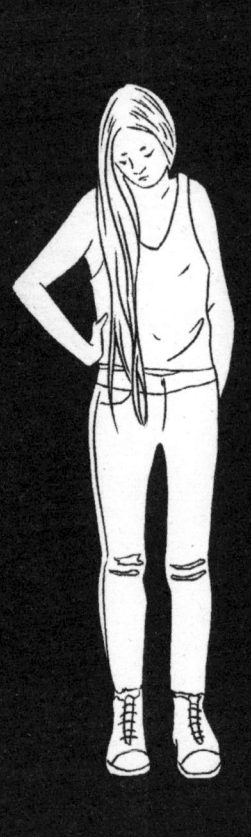

maybe just raw. racing,

a mind that won't stop racing,

at times, ready for an uproar.

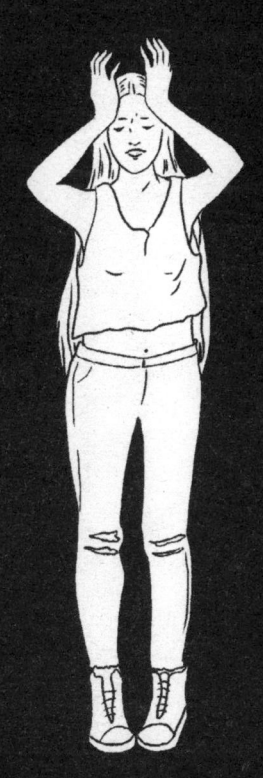

every insomnia makes you the villain.

how do you say, these are the ways depression

shreds me into mini-episodes

of tender and exposed.

Father Where?

Brother sleeps
Mother prays
Brother hides from the law
Brother busted lip
Brother dislocated jaw
Mother prays
Mother prays
Brother bunks school
Brother sagging pants to be cool
Mother prays
Brother fails another year
Mother prays
Brother steals
Brother deals
Mother prays
Mother prays

Brother headaches
Brother x-rays
Brother relapse
Brother rehab
Brother released
Brother redeemed
Brother jailed
Brother bailed
Brother baptised
Brother backslides
Brother high
Mother hallelujah
Mother prays
Mother fasts
Mother kneels
Mother pleads: *our father who art missing*
Father please.
Father be.

Sea Legs

You will sometimes be lodged
between a

                ripple   and   a   rock.

You will be the frailest sort of thing

trying to look graceful in a

                 r   i   p   tide,

no one teaches you how to   g l i d e
in an emergency.

Manual or not, you will realise that
going with the flow often means

                                       surrendering.

At times, you will be an

in-breath

looking for an

out-breath,

a wave reaching for the shore
purges what it no longer needs.

Feel it all:

flotsam and jetsam.

Being OK with being lost is how we
notate the present.

Put your hand on your heart;
this too is a compass.

Weighing-In

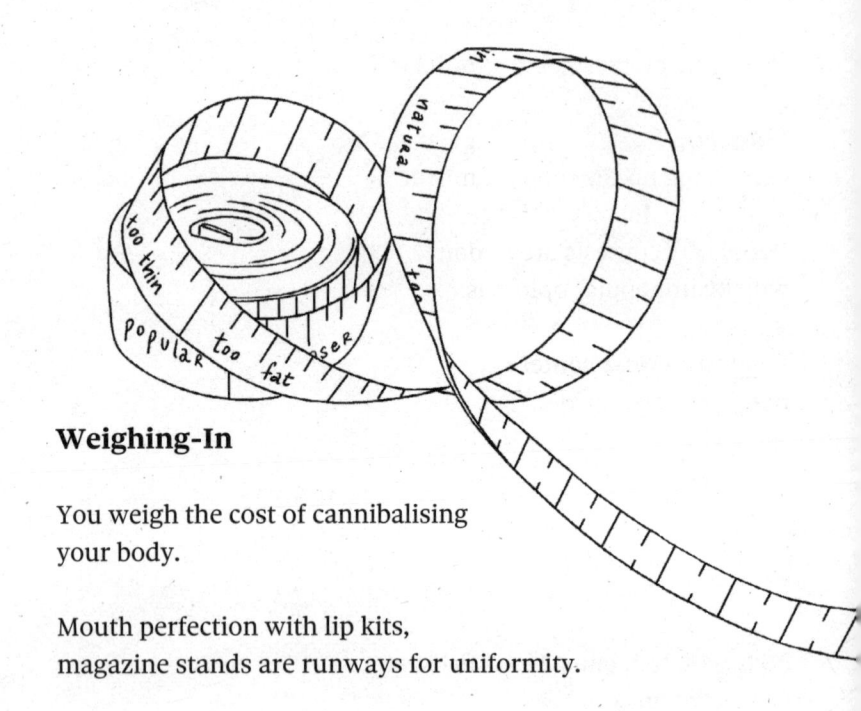

You weigh the cost of cannibalising
your body.

Mouth perfection with lip kits,
magazine stands are runways for uniformity.

The *girls next door*
look nothing like your neighbours.

Everyone is jealous of everyone else
curating their makeup through a screen.

We measure desire,

squeeze and stretch
one size so it fits all.

Fold the edges of our margins
so we can be counted in,

twist our tongues neatly around transformation.

Inclusivity tips the scales in your favour,
depending on the room or mirror.

Popularity contests are seldom
won by unpopular opinions.

You must create content
that is relatable,

you must be content,
be relatable.

Ordinary is not a filter.

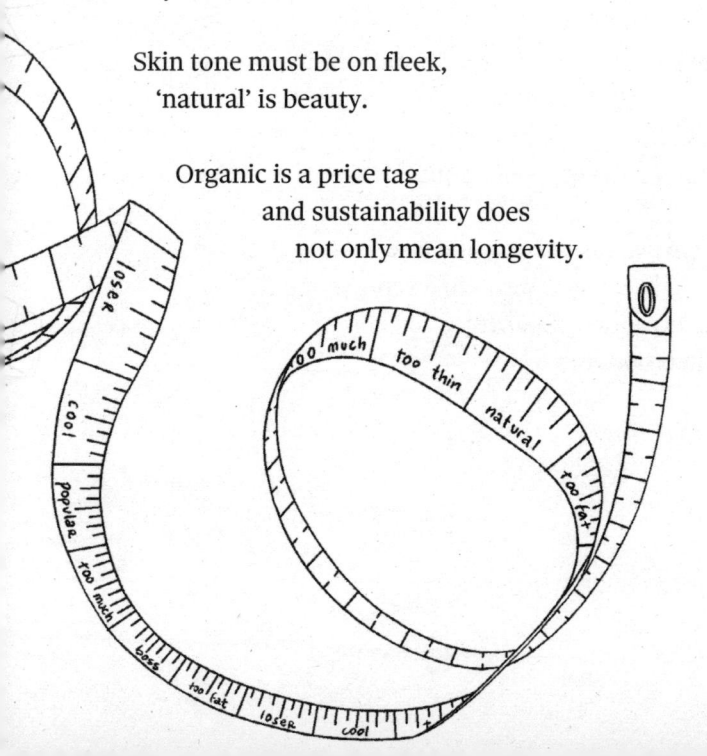

    Skin tone must be on fleek,
      'natural' is beauty.

        Organic is a price tag
            and sustainability does
                not only mean longevity.

Elastic

There are days
when I am at my lowest.

There are days
when help has not felt close enough,

even with one hand s t   r   e   t   c   h   e   d   out.

I worry about tomorrow,
and tomorrow's worries.

I carry failures
that cannot be measured by how much

I tried my best.

I try my best
wondering if I am as good enough

as the promises I keep.

I witness terror and absurdity
and still keep singing.

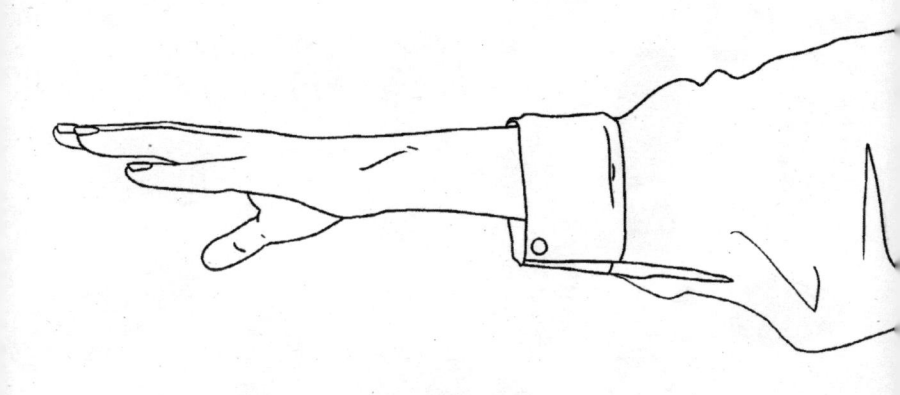

There are days
that marvel at my optimism;

days that affirm my joy,
days that tell me

I am becoming
something worth being proud of.

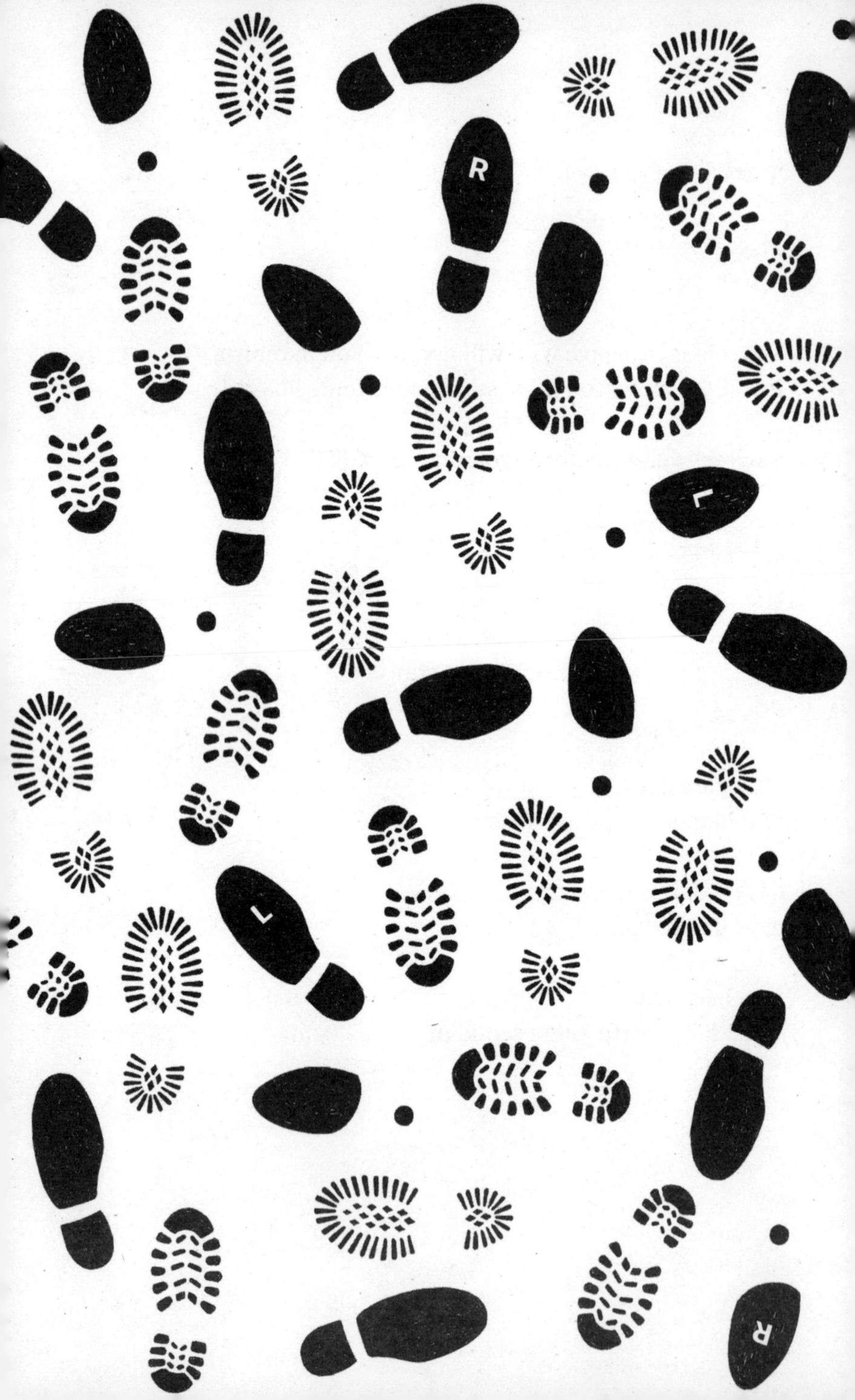
R
L
L
R

Two Left Feet

Places we love the most
can be places that hurt the most.

You will love people who will not love you in return,
it will not mean you must stop loving yourself.

Can I tell you something you may already know:

Truth comes in twos,

and

Fear is a dance you will have to dance
until it feels like your feet belong to you.

Present

I have reached this place
I am afraid to name.

Afraid I will be condemned
if I do not profess his name the way that you
have taught me.

Afraid I will get there
and there will be no heaven or hell.

Afraid that my name won't be written in the
Book of Life
or that the Book of Life has recipes

for those who already know how to live.

I am afraid of the non-existent
yet I know something exists.

I am questioning how I learned to love,
I am questioning how I learned to obey,

I am afraid that I have learned
that obedience is love.

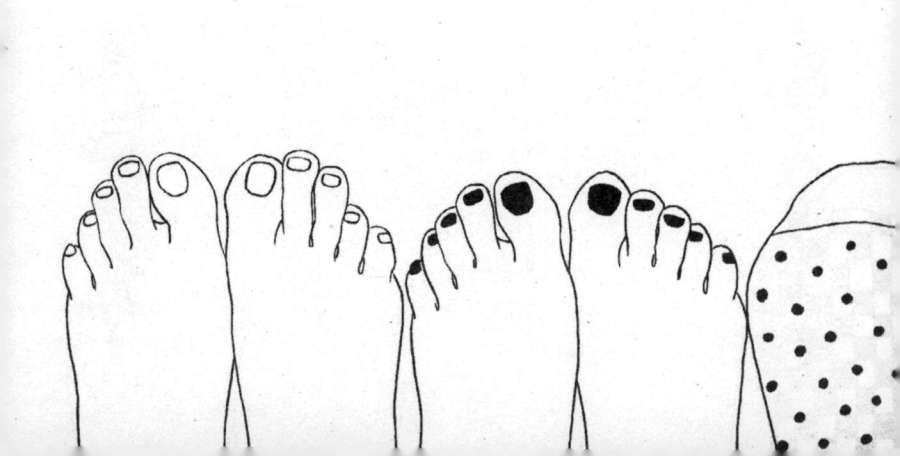

I Thought

if I spoke when I was spoken to,
if I shaped my voice into a sweet quiet squeak,
if I toed the margin,
if I felt pretty enough, I'd feel good enough,
if I tip-toed around the grievance,
if I didn't call the ache what it was,
if I didn't name who caused it,
if I didn't point to the rot,
if I worked hard enough,
if I only mattered in ways that made me matter,
it would buy my place in the family of things.

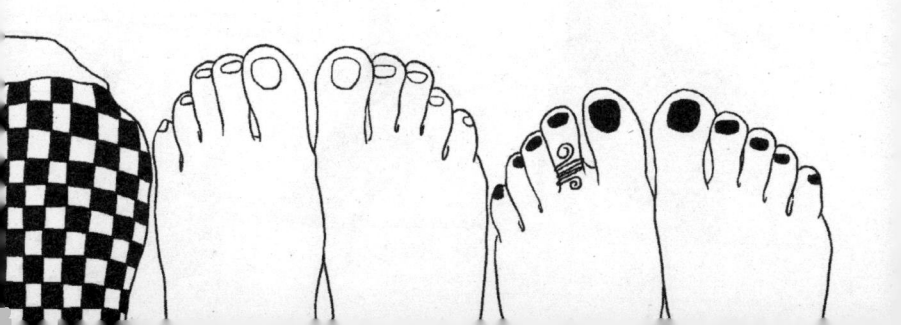

Uprising

The constitution is revised
while the revolution is being televised.

Realities are disguised
with half-truths improvised.

The story is canonised
with a history that is summarised.

Be careful of what is advertised
when brutality has been stylised.

The people cannot be unionised
when the system has them polarised.

The dream is always incentivised
so that capitalism can thrive.

They devise ways to deprive us of time.

Teachings

Away from drip and cool
Away from figures in stilettos and glossy lips
Away from poles and mysterious corners
Away from margins that make centres rot

Away from leeches that leave you leaking
Away from touching and feeling
Away from observers
Away from grown-up people's microscopes

Away from foul-mouthed hip-hop and trap
Away from taboos that make you less curious
Away from the boogeymen never seen but always talked about
Away from secret accounts that account for our secrets

Away from encrypted files and corrupted data
Away from the corrupt and spine-chilling
Away from noise makers who stir trouble
Away from packs and herds and groupies

Away from fansONLY

Away from those who live double lives
Away from those who live lives that are not neat and tidy.

You fear

(maybe *question* instead of *fear*)

You question

(maybe *I* instead of *you*)

I question all the forbiddens that were never explained
They are so afraid to name a sword a portal
They leave ~~me~~ us penetrable.

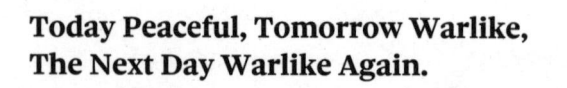

Today Peaceful, Tomorrow Warlike, The Next Day Warlike Again.

It begins on the coast
shorelines submerged in conflict and ceasefire.

Those who do not have tongues to trade
negotiate with their bodies.

Swindlers settle inland
identifying trespassers.

Millionaires and moguls
harvest to hoard;

uprooting indigenous practices
in the interest of conservation.

Conquest hunts and grabs
and never asks for permission

or forgiveness.

The Wild Coast Seabed recalls
the Ogoni in Niger Delta.

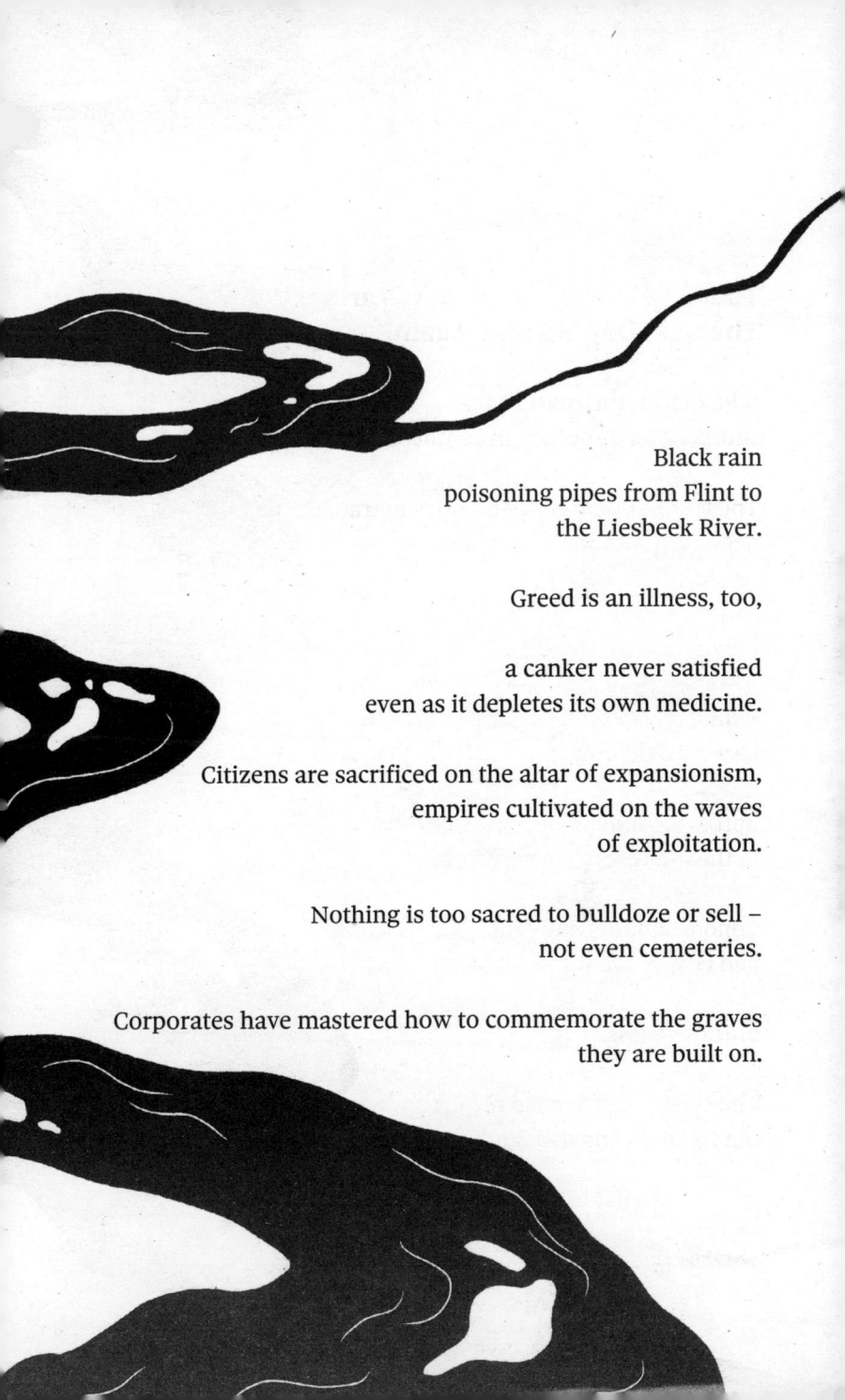

Black rain
poisoning pipes from Flint to
the Liesbeek River.

Greed is an illness, too,

a canker never satisfied
even as it depletes its own medicine.

Citizens are sacrificed on the altar of expansionism,
empires cultivated on the waves
of exploitation.

Nothing is too sacred to bulldoze or sell –
not even cemeteries.

Corporates have mastered how to commemorate the graves
they are built on.

Paying respect to First Nations
and ongoing custodians of the land
does not count as reparations.

They will always find money
for surveillance and war.

We are not too young
to operate artillery or barricade doors;

militaries have training grounds in
classrooms and churches, too,

and airstrikes do not wait
for amen.

They pledge allegiance to a flag
always raised at half-mast for its children.

The largest exporter of violence
asks for gun control laws

when 45,000 lives are massacred
on 750 military bases in 80 countries.

We have been to so many vigils.
We have become so many vigils.

We have been to so many protests.
We have become so many protests,

    holding up the weight of
    tomorrow's sorrow.

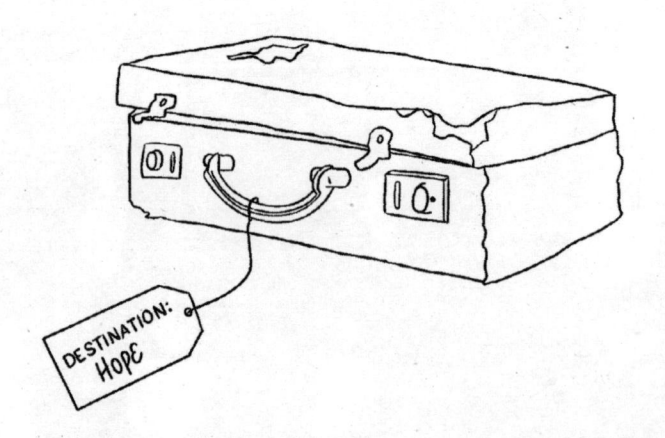

Refuge
Noun

Some of us know of hope
that is pinned on crossing borders.

Banned/Burned

We are citizens ceaselessly surveilled
but not safeguarded.

Kept under the watch of the state, the police,
big tech has us glued to our screens.

We are terminally online,
rely on technologies to tether us to the Earth, to each other.

We accept cookies in exchange for access.

We are lured by candy
that leaves us vulnerable and exposed;

nothing is given freely
even when it is free.

An army of censors dictates

what is seen
what is heard
what is read

who is seen
who is heard
who is read.

There is evidence for everything,
even when they shut down the internet.

History,

with its sharp tusks,
its thorny jewels,
its appetite for memory,

moves through time as elephants do.

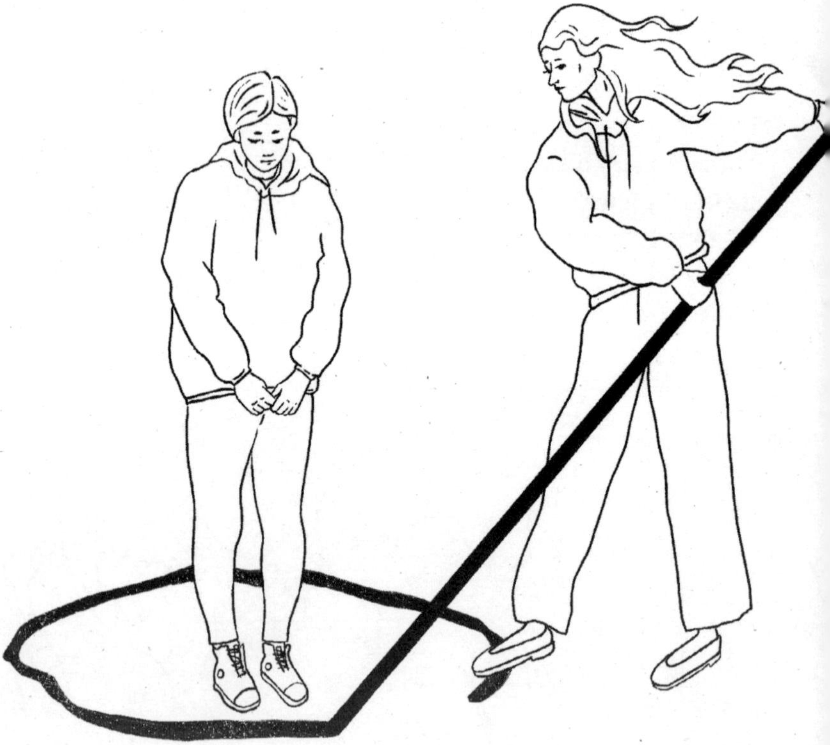

Boundaries

You allow people to shit on you long enough
you start believing you stink.

Passage

Tongues and tyres
are not the only things torched

in our country
everything burns.

Arson signaling an abscess.

Riots on the outskirts
boil over and into a city centre
veneered for tourists.

In the riot, a stampede shields
a baby thrown from a building on fire.

Temples of learning and living
swollen shut by our chronic pyromania.

We have been intimate with fires for too long.

The Railway Depot furnace at Kaserne, Johannesburg
provides an index of music and books

burned at municipal incinerators
under the Customs Act of 1955,

archival documents compressed in trucks
from Pretoria's Central Police Station to the furnaces of Iscor,

volumes of censored shelves
dropped into a 20-metre-high oven –

testimonials whistling into smoke.

Lost libraries that were never logged as history,
as fact.

What is feared most by those in power
can be found in the spines they break.

26,000 books were banned under the Publications Act of 1974,
contraband funneled through broken telephones.

Reading has always been incendiary

under the Riotous Assemblies Act of 1930,
under the Suppression of Communism Act of 1950,
under the Public Safety Act of 1953,

we find

an index of texts lost,
an index of texts out of print,

an index of texts buried,
an index of texts drowned,

an index of all that remains;

we remember everything
the fires could not erase.

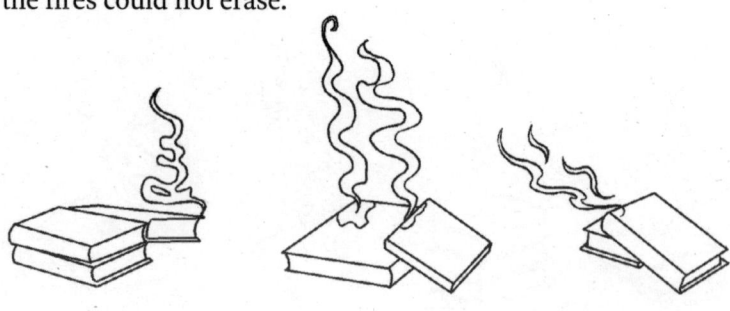

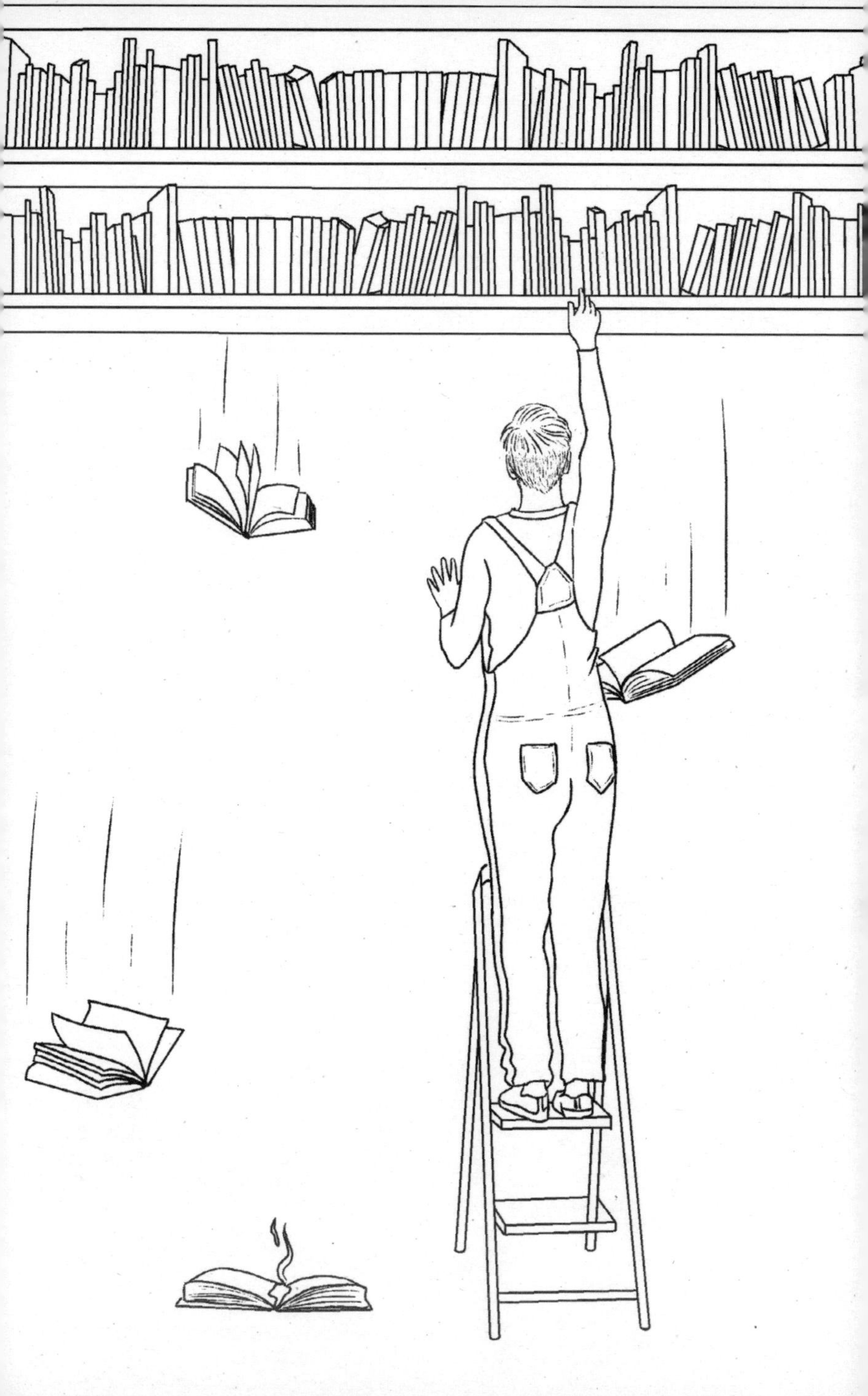

Part 3

. . . then tomorrow.

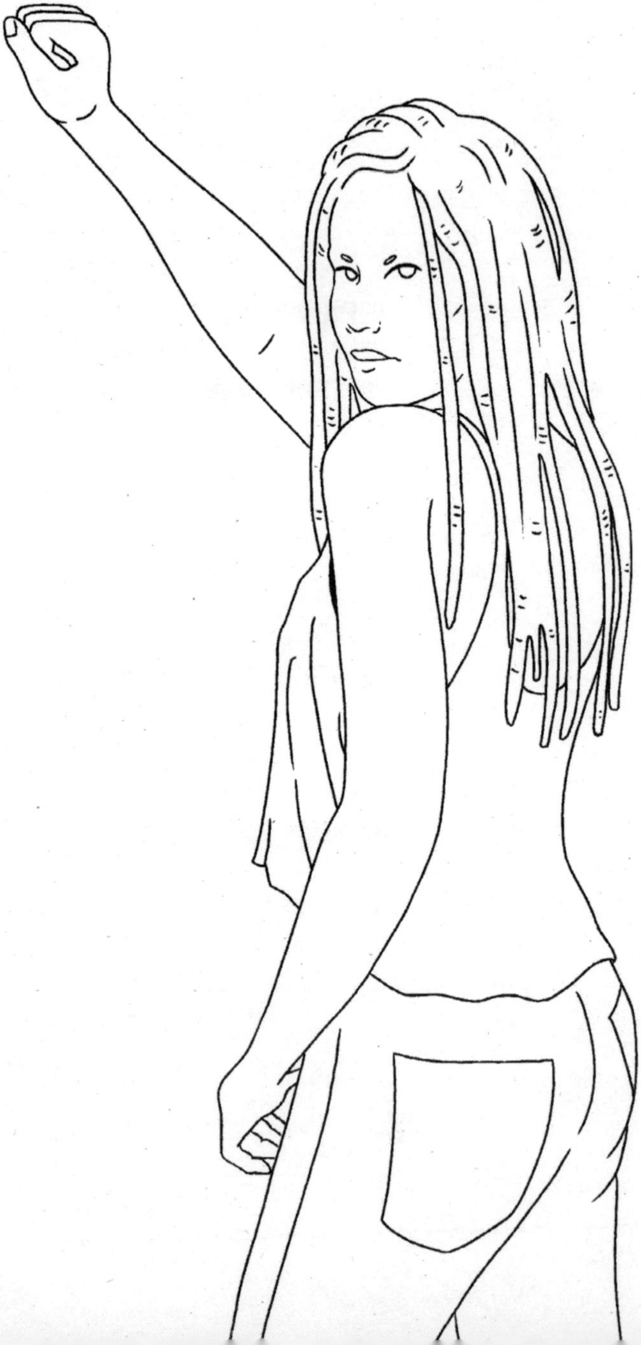

History

We don't want a History that keeps us from the world we want to see.
We don't want a History that keeps us from seeing how much more we could be.

We don't want a History that sits on the fence.
We don't want a History that always speaks,

and never listens.

We don't want a History that chokes when we speak it.
We don't want a History that doesn't acknowledge what came before it.

We don't want a History that loops around its mistakes.
We don't want a History that learns too late

the ~~error~~ fate of its ways.

We don't want a History that keeps the oppressed from being free.
We don't want a History that keeps us from the world we want to see.

Homecoming

You are allowed to figure it out as you figure it out,
there are no wrong turns,

only cul de sacs that reveal what you haven't considered
or ways of returning.

There will always be *somewhere* to return to,
even if that *somewhere* does not want us in return.

Protégé or Prototype

We are thick skin
and plant-based ideals,

digital natives
at the forefront of information.

We learn coding to challenge the system.
We align with brands that share our beliefs.

We are not afraid to press our palms against power
and push back.

We could teach you how to
hack roadblocks in Roblox.

We are gamers imagining new worlds,
we inhabit more than one reality.

We have the entirety
of mankind's possibilities in our pockets,

we can gain access
with a single

click.

We take heartbreak on the chin,

ink our sins,
call death by suicide what it is.

We are creators and innovators,
we change the world from our bedrooms.

We obey rules by breaking them,
nod to old traditions while inventing new rituals.

We know the cost of being neighbours with our planet.
Upcycling is how we give second chances.

We are overthinkers and overachievers
who give themselves permission to be

heathens and believers.

We have more than one shot
to convert our wishes.

School is not the only
stream where we learn how to swim.

We learn how to dream
by treading water.

</digitalnatives)

<props> <value>

class = " InkOurSins_ ComplexObject)"
<!-wearegamersimaginingnewworlds.properties)call-->
eliefs>

"administrator">administrator palms againts power </prop>
</click>

<prop key= " believers" > <va
</props>
</pushback>
<!-results treadingwater(java.util.list) call--> <list>
="wishes">
<reality>
<value>obeyrulesbybreakingthem</value>
<bean id ="moreComplexObject" school ="example.ComplexObject">
-resultsInaSetWehavemoreThanOne.shot)call-->

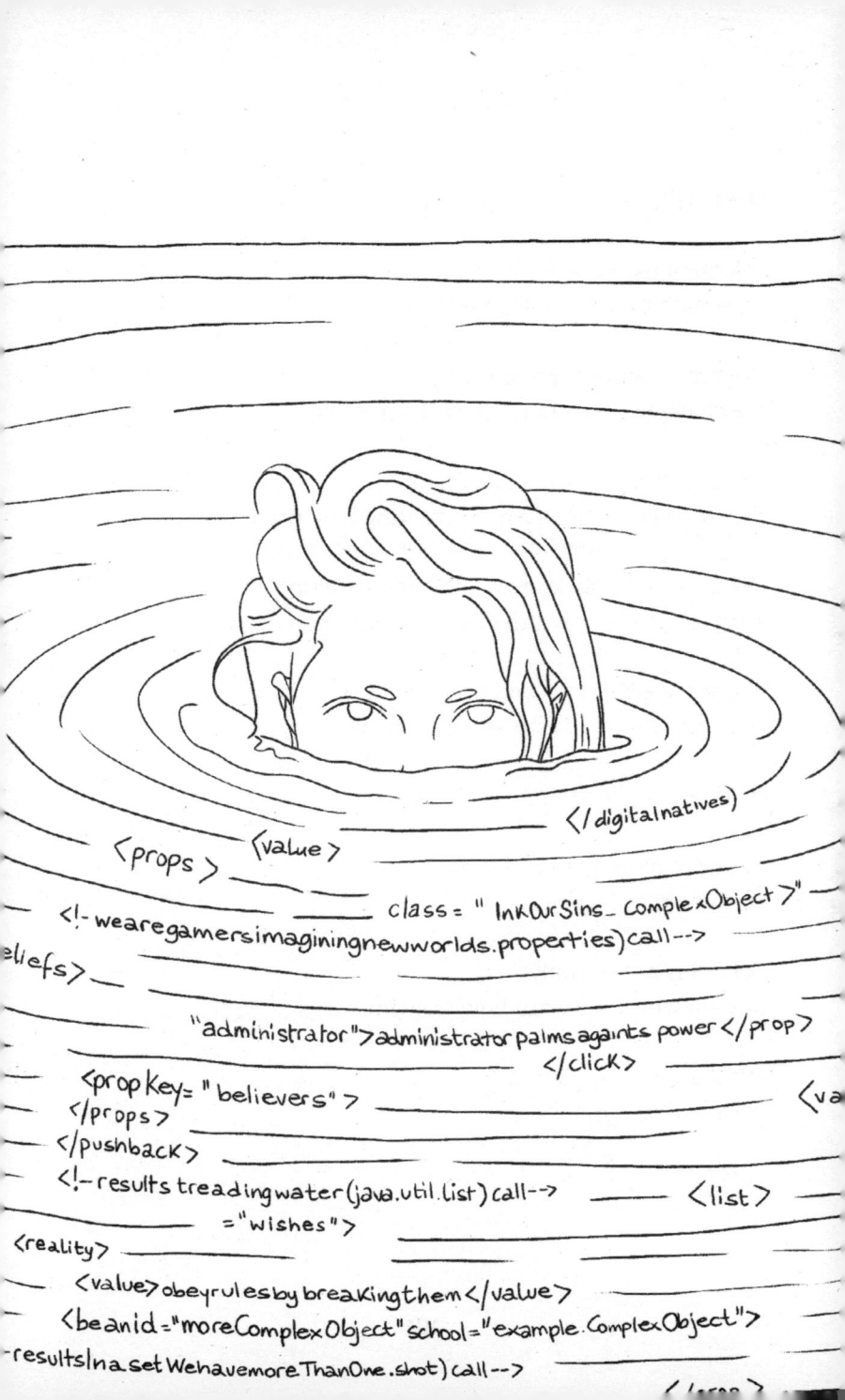

Kid Gloves

The woes of the world
and my rage often feel intertwined.

I have to remind myself
to put my fists down.

I am love, I know love.

And even this does not mean that anger is not present.
Rage is sometimes a love's need to grieve.

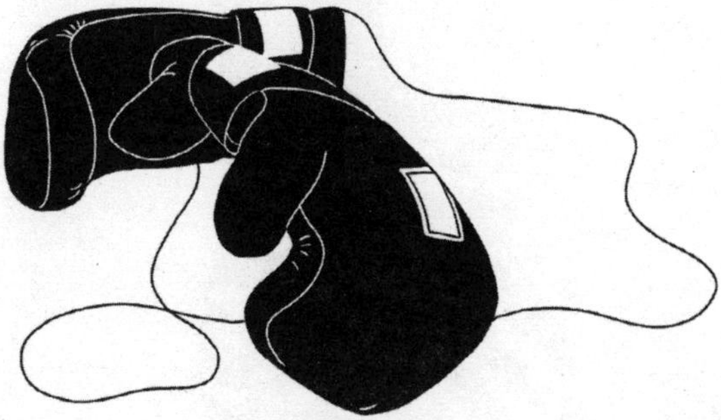

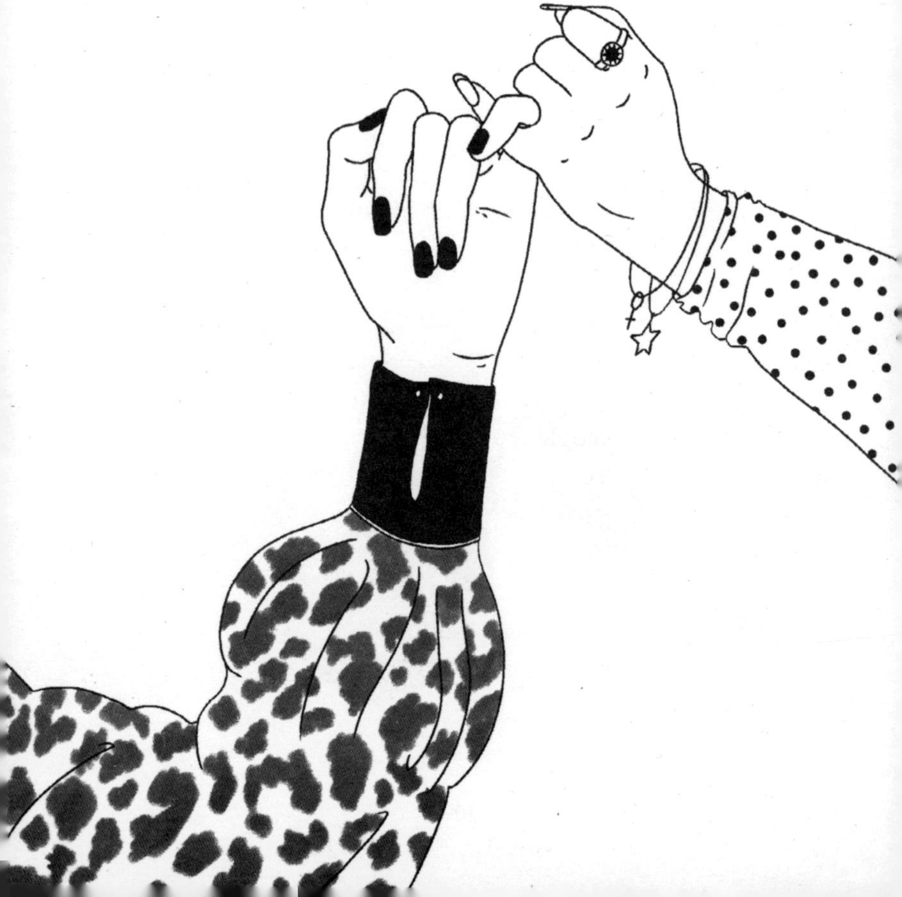

Pinky Promise

On our grandmothers' past lives
we vow to always be best friends,

to honour bedtime
with FaceTime and honesty,

to be familiar nooks and crannies
when everything else is unfamiliar.

Our secrets are our bond,
we know where all the bodies are buried.

Here,

we do not have to conceal the parts of ourselves
we feel most ashamed of.

We are each other's utopia,
each other's safe place.

When we find our people
it can feel as if we are

surrounded by mirrors.

Unlearning

I was born into a body that learned how to use fear as a compass,
tells me where to look,

how to say grace with all eyes open.

I want to unlearn:
being afraid of everything.

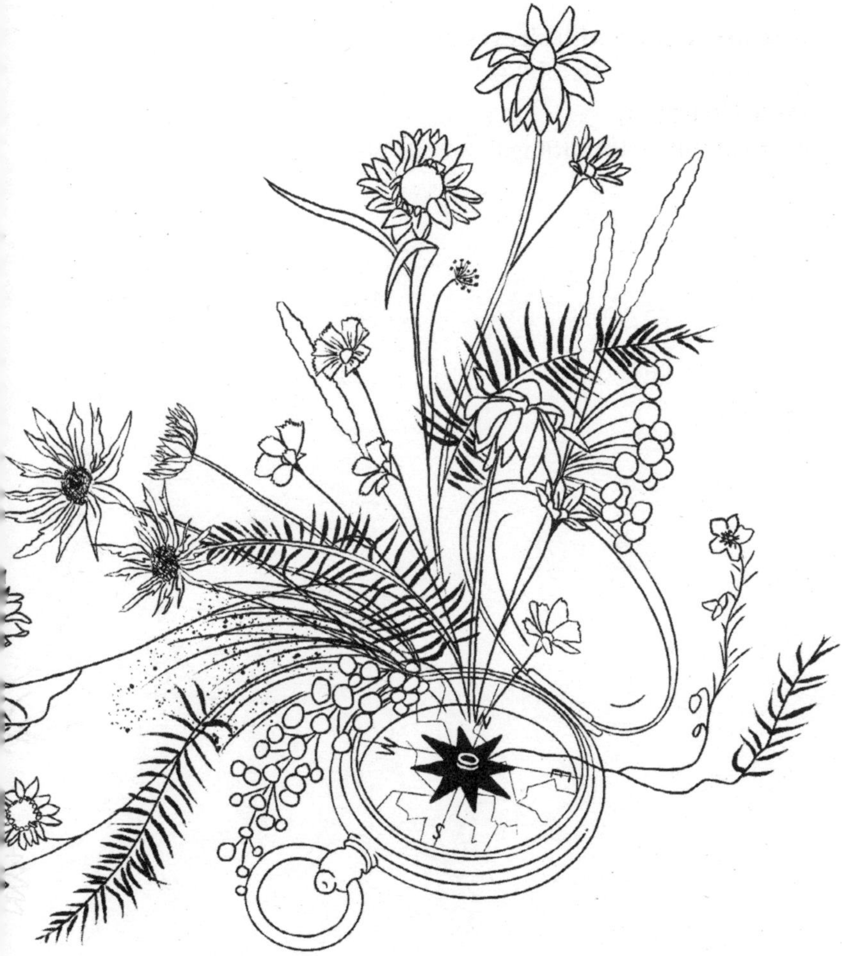

Speak!

Speak!
Earsplitting and sharp,
summon their ears to hearken.

Speak!
With your throat trembling,
tongue-twisting,
mouth waving frantically in a murmur.

It is nerve-racking,
(I know).

But speak!
Say it with your chest
wide open,

with your lungs
levitating,

your hands
shaking,

your knees
jiggling,

your passageways
creaking,

your voice
exiting your lips on tiptoe.

It is nerve-racking,
(I know).

Inhale   and   exhale,
if you must.

When you are ready,
we are ready to hear you

s p e a k!

Pause

more silence,
more surrendering to the unknown
to the flow of things,

more listening,
more looking to see what is being looked at,

more fearless love,
more showing up for oneself,
for the communities that need us to care more deeply,

more empathy,

more honesty about the sadness we carry,
and all the losses we cannot carry alone,

more laughter from the farthest corners of our joys,
more curiosity,
more solitude and ease,

more feeling,
not just with touch

but all our senses,

and the sixth,
and seventh,

and the ones we acquire by living,

by feeling,

more 'us' and 'we' (together),

more guts to shoot our shot
believing we deserve every beautiful thing,

more grace for our mistakes,

more care,
more questions,

more openness to try
even when we don't feel ready or good enough,

more love,
we can never love enough,

more compassion for ourselves,
each other,

more dancing,
we can never dance enough,

more space for our collective rage,
there are so many injustices that need it,

more pause when life humbles us.

You are still here.
We are still here.

F is for Forgiveness

F is for how fond a heart can be of things we cannot have.

F is for fam,

Fam is for 'someplace familiar'.

Somewhere familiar won't always ask for your forgiveness.

F is for the forgiveness we give to free ourselves.

SoundCloud

Fingers on the pulse,
K-pop blended in Korean and English,
downbeat-electronic, lo-fi music with a lot of heart,
bluegrass, reggae and space rock.

You
Pimp a Butterfly
Happier Than Ever.

You are descendants of vinyl and cassettes,
iPods making waves for AirPods.

Before Bluetooth
enabled a wireless connection,

you were the latest drop.
Continue to make pop culture
pop, lock, and drop.

Top the charts,
make the blues nostalgic.

Live as you feel.

You're as big as Little Simz,
as big as
Big Freedia making booties Bounce in a Beyoncé video.

You create your own label,
move with genres that define your sound,

you are redemption songs
and songs of freedom.

Odyssey

you are small
how aware of your smallness you are

you are big
how committed to your bigness you are

flesh that still has so much to give
flesh that holds a restless and anxious spirit

flesh that wakes and sleeps, wanders, and wanders
in search of the next

you have secrets that make you lie,
and lies

that make you live outside of your truth.
truth is

we are all lopsided, winging it,
flailing. release yourself

from your own judgement.
you know how.

let your heart go, then
your hips, then
your neck.

when you are stiff around the shoulder blades,
peel them back.

the beginning of the journey is the hardest.

be patient with becoming,
the answers are in the questions.

sometimes

it hurts where it's healing.

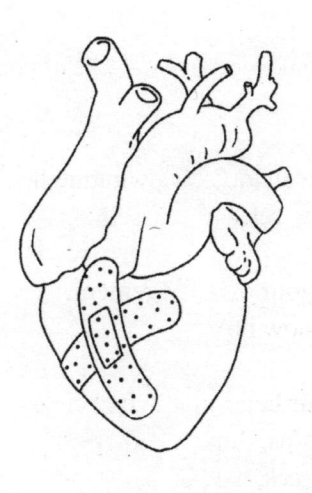

Meteor (or Masculinity)

When they ask you
what do you want to be when you grow up,

say:

sensitive,

soft,

aware.

They will mistake you
for grown

when you grow up
two feet ahead of your time.

When they ask you
what makes you a man,

say:

feeling.

Some days
you will feel like the night sky,

vast and endless.

Sometimes
you will feel the weight of expectation

trying to box you in.

On those days
look up and remember.

What makes you a man
is everything that makes you human

and spirit.

Choice Assorted

I search unmarked doors to locate where I come from;
history is already there when I arrive.

I come from photographs neatly tucked away
and brought out to show visitors.

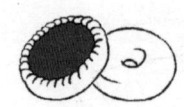

I come from curfews marked by sunsets.

I come from long road trips
with finger-licking good

in the back seat

singing and bopping along to bumps
and humps –

things were always smoother
in stillness.

I come from Aunty So-and-so's
sugar and milk that were never in shortage.

Choice Assorted biscuits and fireworks
reserved for special occasions;

we were the special occasion.

Where I come from
everyone ~~was~~ is your cousin.

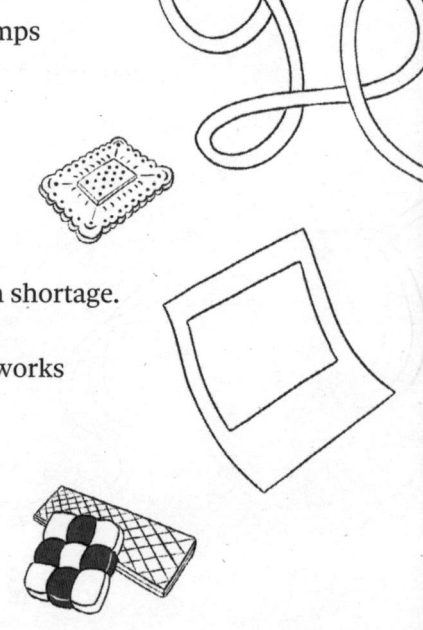

Uncles
gambled with things they were afraid to lose.

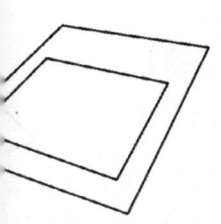

Mothers
took care of things they loved.

Prophets
wore shiny shoes and held your gaze for too long.

Neighbours
greeted in high-pitched voices and fed everyone playing in their yard.

Grandmothers
neatly folded and tucked plastic bags in the bottom drawer.

Grandfathers
read philosophy books and cooked spicy food after midnight.

Tin cans clapped in percussion,
feet jumped rope.

Rhythm in an endless loop.

Joy was here and
joy was next door.

It said good morning
and it made sure to always say goodnight.

Roll Call

I go unnoticed until
I stall in an aisle,

it is assumed I cannot afford
what is in front of me.

I feel out of place
in all the places I am different.

I feel displaced
in all the places home is gentrified.

I have come to think

there must be a world
where going unnoticed is an invitation

to see myself.

Twenty-One Ways to Check Your Pulse

1. Hallowed be thy name,
you are the story that has survived the killings of darlings.

      2. Hallowed be your name,
      your will is your power.

      Let it carry you into tomorrow.

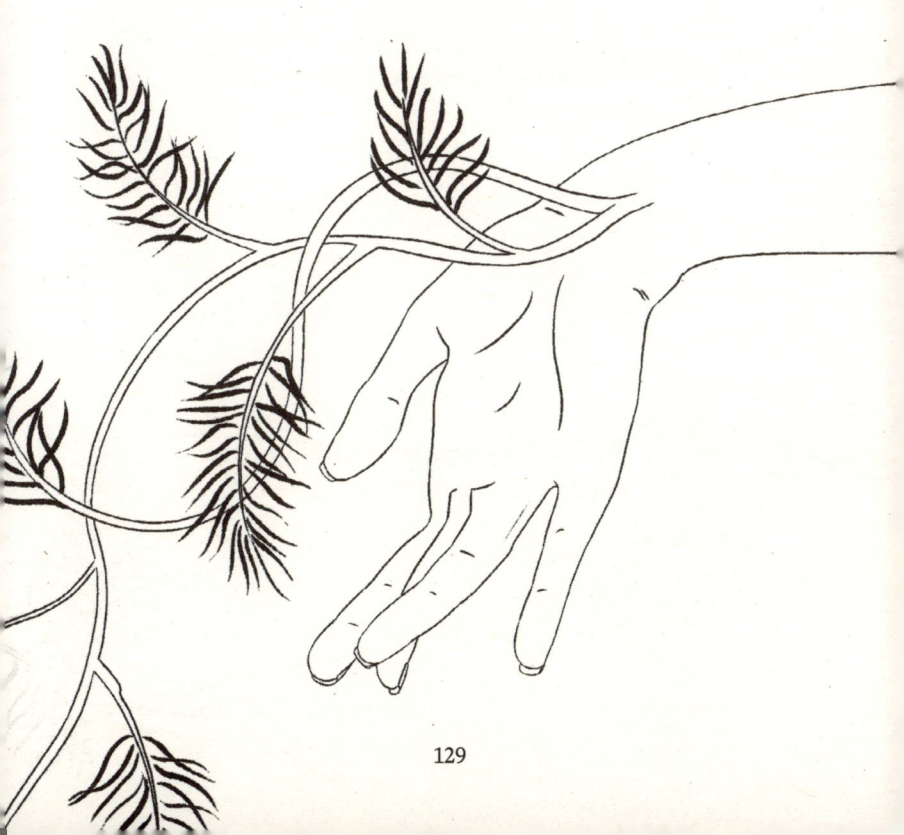

3.   We are loneliest when we are tired.
We become weary when we've been strong for too long.

4.   You have hardened where you have broken.
You are bravest in all your tender places.

5.   You deserve beautiful karma,
the luck of the universe's draw.

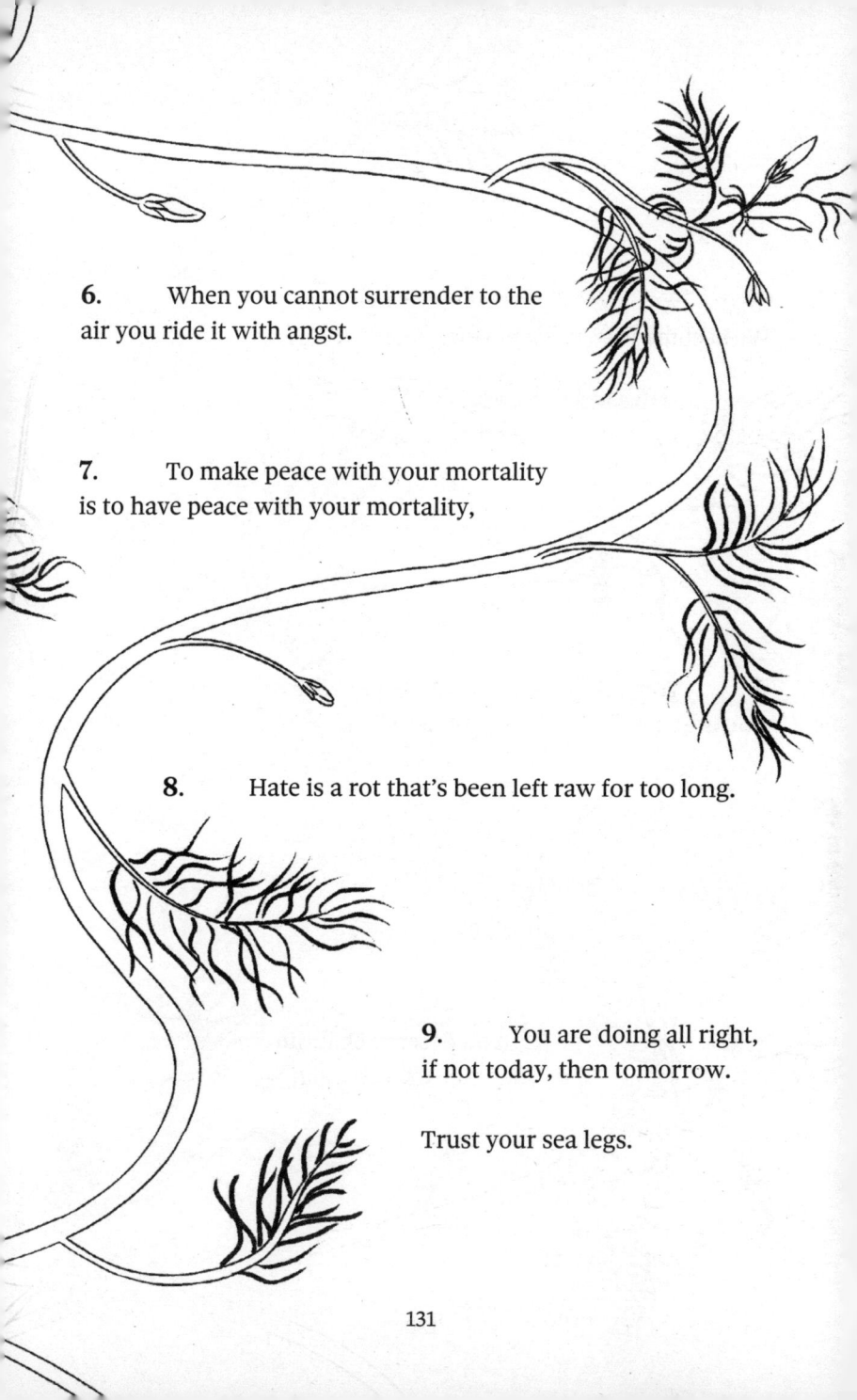

6. When you cannot surrender to the air you ride it with angst.

7. To make peace with your mortality is to have peace with your mortality,

8. Hate is a rot that's been left raw for too long.

9. You are doing all right, if not today, then tomorrow.

Trust your sea legs.

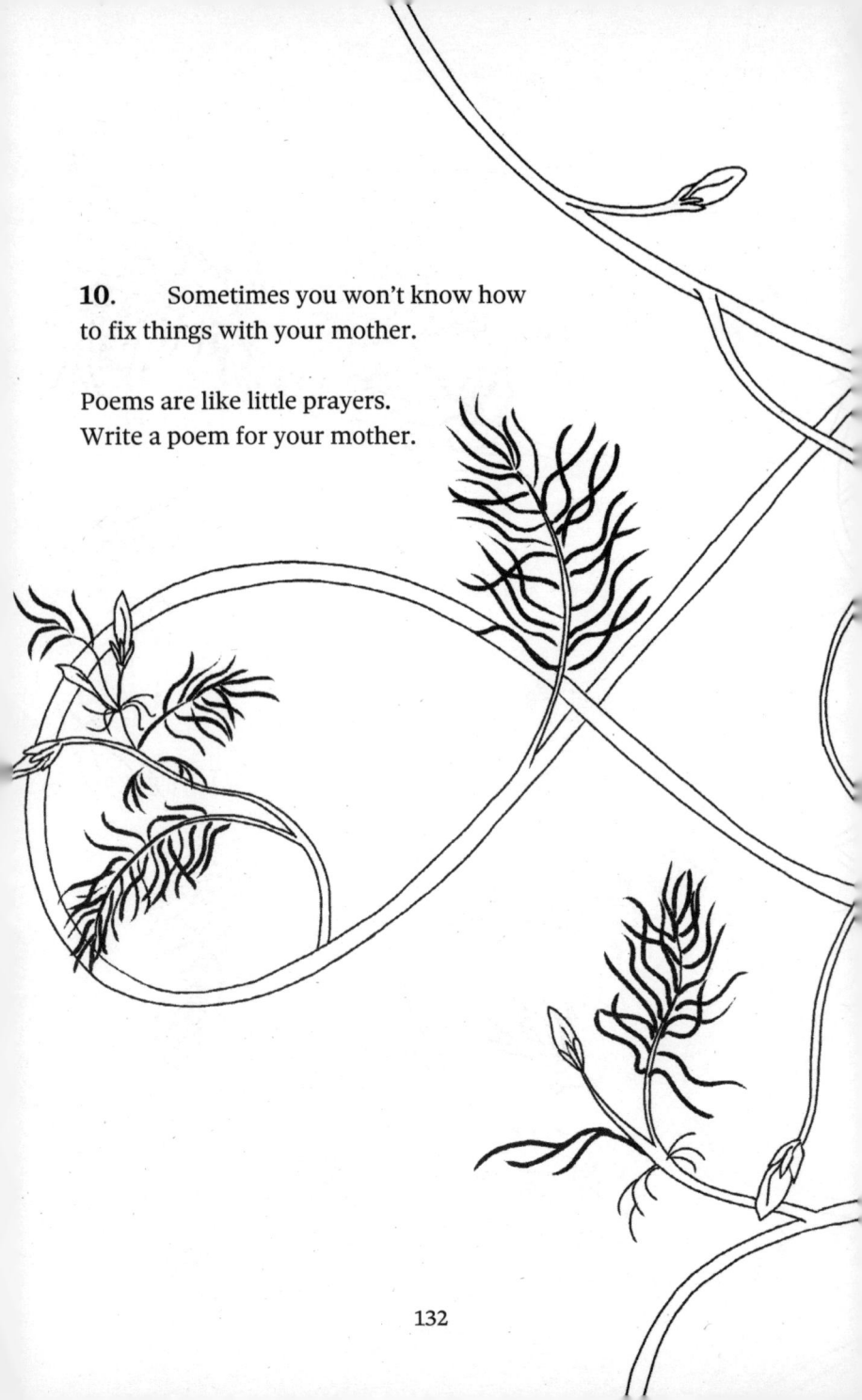

10. Sometimes you won't know how
to fix things with your mother.

Poems are like little prayers.
Write a poem for your mother.

11. Make room for lighter things.

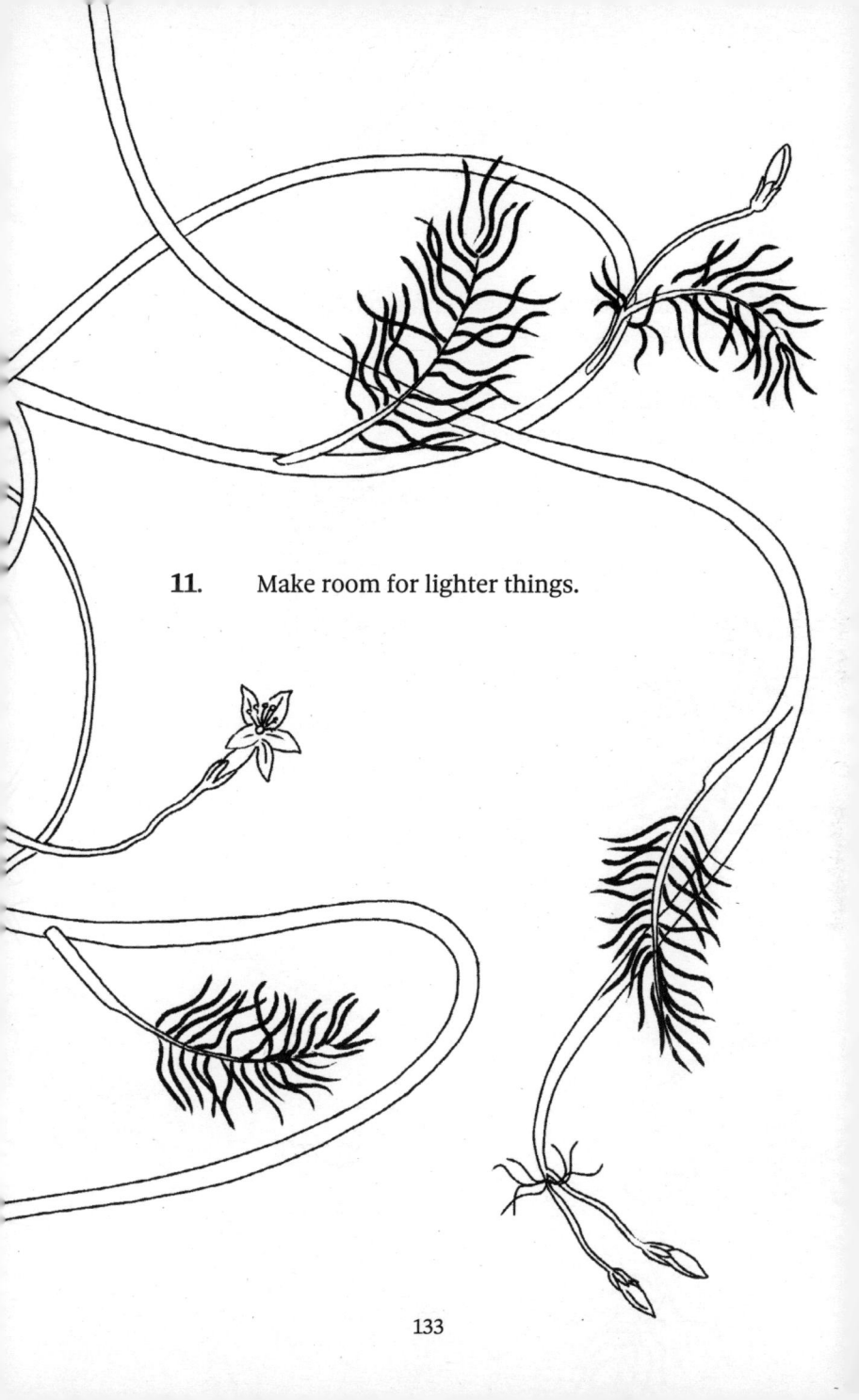

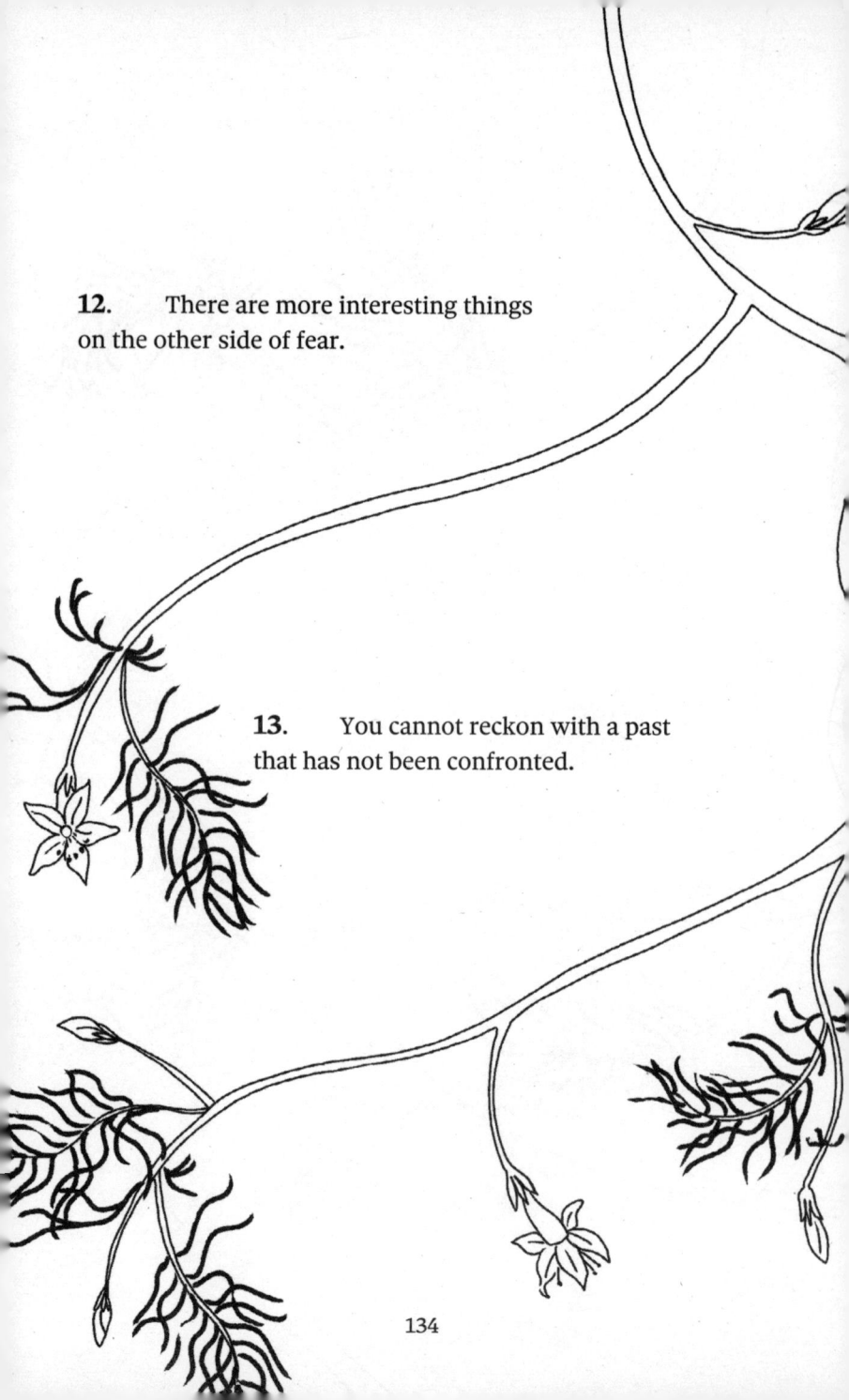

12. There are more interesting things on the other side of fear.

13. You cannot reckon with a past that has not been confronted.

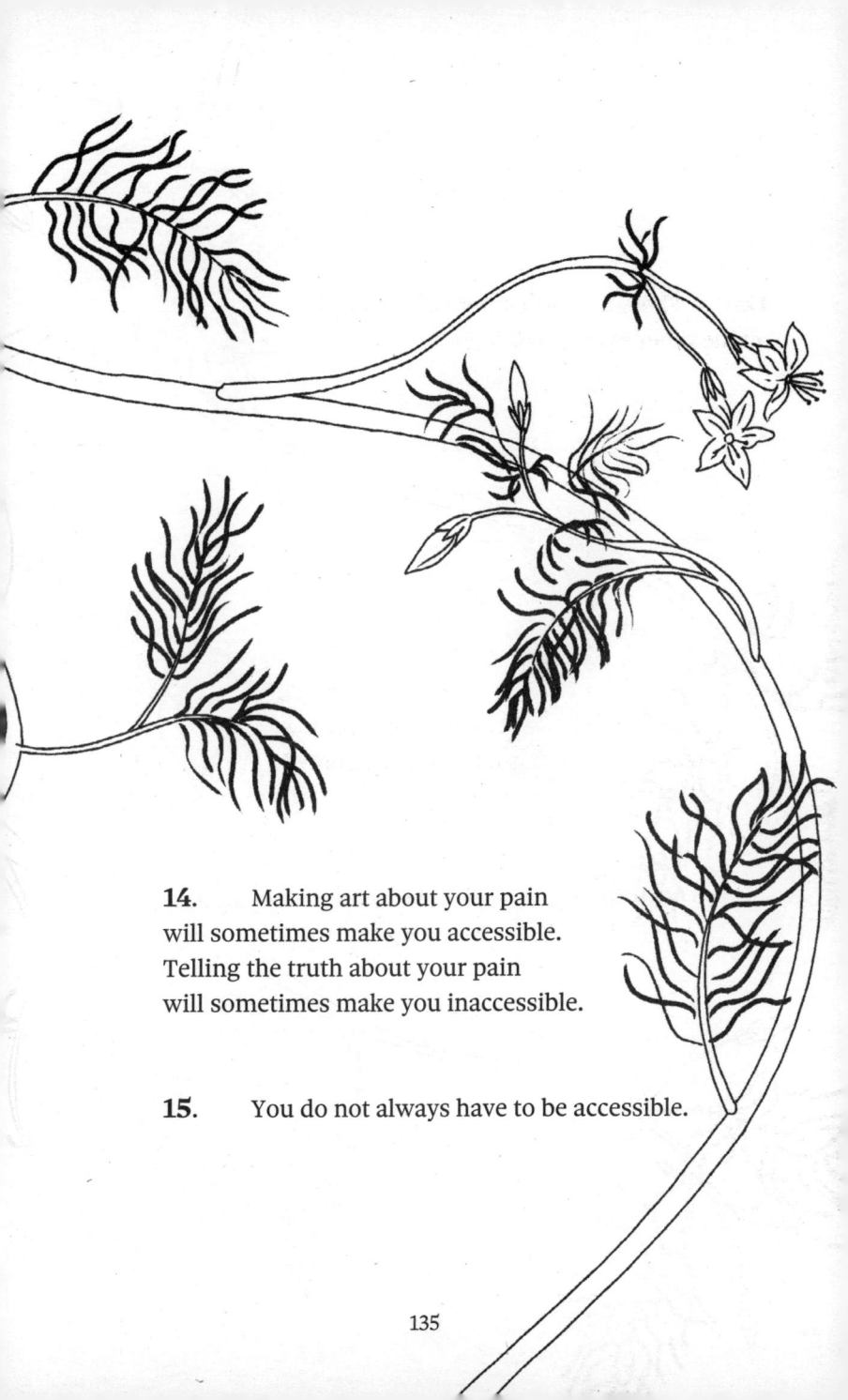

14.   Making art about your pain
will sometimes make you accessible.
Telling the truth about your pain
will sometimes make you inaccessible.

15.   You do not always have to be accessible.

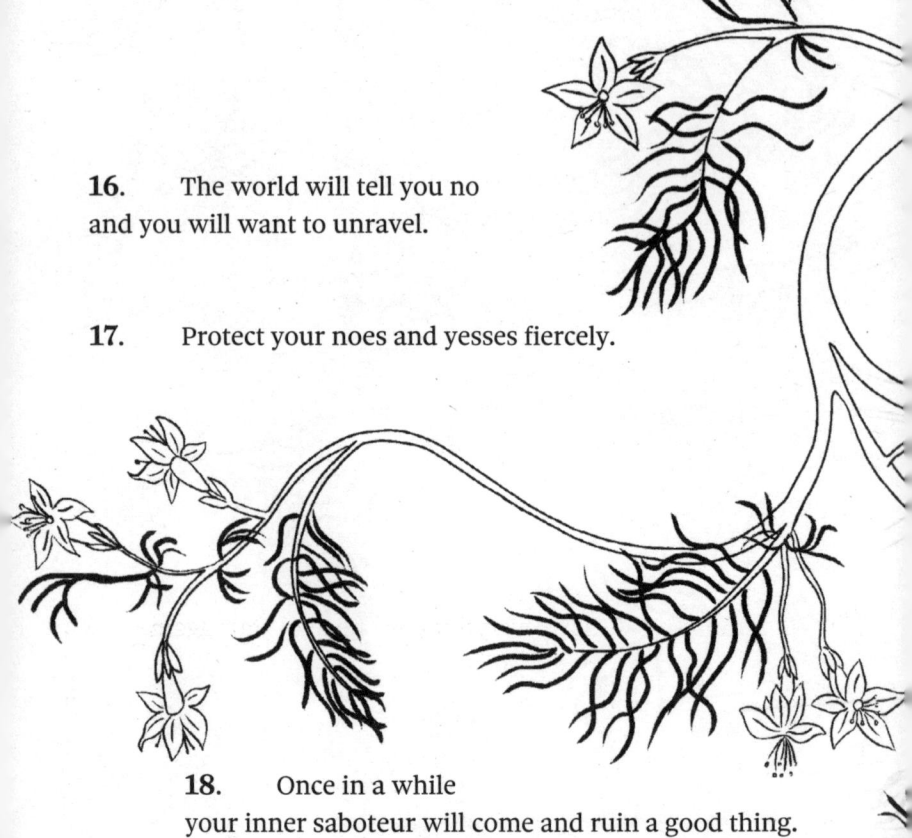

16.   The world will tell you no
and you will want to unravel.

17.   Protect your noes and yesses fiercely.

18.   Once in a while
your inner saboteur will come and ruin a good thing.

19.   You, wild heart, are every good thing,
remember this.

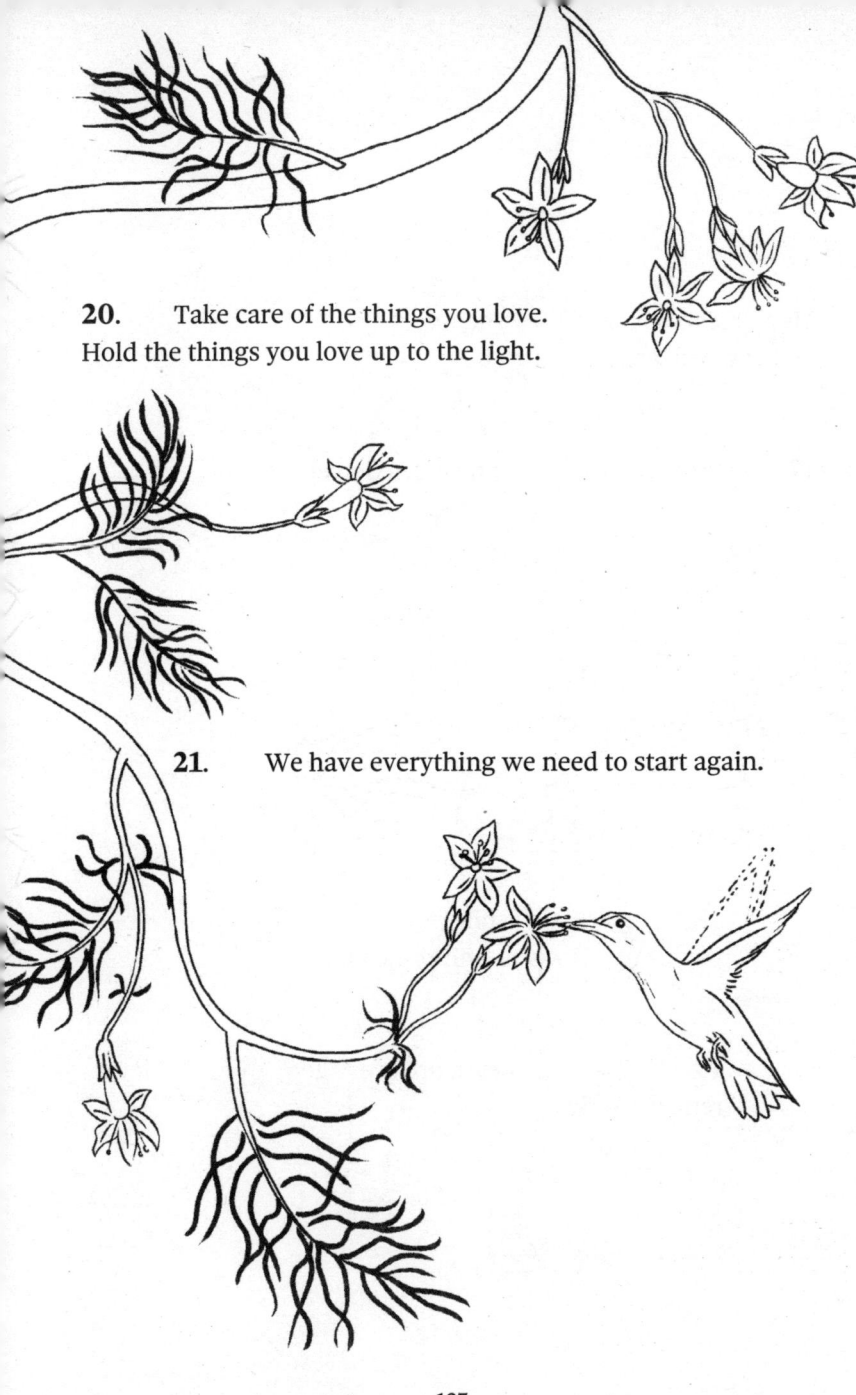

20. Take care of the things you love.
Hold the things you love up to the light.

21. We have everything we need to start again.

Praise Poem

You blink around twenty times a minute.

There are eight thousand taste buds enveloping your tongue
and your ears never stop growing.

You are a constellation of miracles.

Your heart pumps two thousand five hundred gallons
of blood every day,

it never tires.

The closing and opening of the heart's valves
is the beating sound we hear.

If you smoothed out all the wrinkles,
your brain would look flat like a pillowcase.

Three hundred million balloon-like structures known as alveoli
could make your lungs float on water.

You can float on water.

Press both feet to the ground.
Place your hand on your heart.

You are brave and capable.

        It will always be your time.

Epilogue

We are the light at the   end   of   the   tunnel.

Author's Note

Never in my wildest dreams did I think I would be a published poet, much less the author of a whole poetry collection. Writing has been my lifeline since I fell in love with words and writing at the age of fourteen. I hope that these poems will provide the reader with the same sense of comfort and belonging that reading a book or poem still does for me. I still feel, in many ways, that I am attempting to pay tribute to my fourteen-year-old self – her bravery, her radical faith in the transformative power of poetry and her desire to use language to connect with the outside world and other people. This book is for you as much as it is for her.

I hope what you are looking for has already found you.

Acknowledgements

Even though writing can be a solitary endeavour, the amount of support and collaboration required to finish a book never ceases to amaze me. I am grateful to my editor, Ella Whiddett, for inspiring this project and for her firm yet kind guidance throughout the process. I will always be appreciative. Thank you to the team at Hot Key Books for all the work and effort that has gone into this project already. I am grateful to Francine Simon for providing a safe space for me to share my ideas and unfinished drafts. Your generosity and notes are with me. Thank you, Robyn, for always taking care of the not-so-little things. Adriana Bellet, our collaboration has made me feel like the luckiest author. Thank you for giving this collection your voice and language. To the OY! Theatre Collective, who sat in a circle with me and answered all of my questions while also sharing bits about themselves, thank you. I will always be grateful for the interactions I had with the most brilliant and beautiful minds – those who attended my workshops, shared their insights and were incredibly kind and honest. Thank you, thank you all.

About the Author

Koleka Putuma is an award-winning South African theatre practitioner, writer and poet. Her bestselling debut poetry collection, *Collective Amnesia*, received the Glenna Luschei Prize for African Poetry, was named Book of the Year by the City Press and was chosen as one of the books of the year by *The Sunday Times* and *Quartz Africa*. Her work tackles themes such as sexuality, gender, race and politics. In 2022 Putuma was awarded the Standard Bank Young Artist Award – the first-time award for poetry. She is also the founder and director of Manyano Media, a multidisciplinary creative company that empowers and produces stories by black queer women. She lives in Cape Town.

About the Illustrator

Adriana Bellet is an illustrator with her heart divided between Spain, Britain and Sweden. She has a degree in advertising but has never used it. She discovered her love for illustration while studying design. She taught herself to draw and developed an obsession with old-school art materials. Still, the iPad is her tool of choice. She is based in Stockholm.